Sustainable Business:
An Executive's Primer

Sustainable Business: An Executive's Primer is extremely interesting and different. The angle of sustainability and community is almost completely absent in any textbook I have reviewed or used. Just reading the Human Resources chapter has started my thinking on the matter.

—Thomas Tudor, Ph.D., University of Arkansas at Little Rock

How excellent for you to be able to put out such a book. I think it is a cutting edge subject.

—Scott Wright, Owner, Century 21 Wright Real Estate

Sustainable Business: An Executive's Primer

Nancy E. Landrum, Ph.D.

Sandra Edwards, Ph.D.

Sustainable Business: An Executive's Primer
Chapter 4: Finance
Author: Julia S. Kwok, Ph.D.
Department of Accounting and Finance
College of Business and Technology
Northeastern State University
3100 E. New Orleans Street
Broken Arrow, OK 74014
E-mail: kwok@nsuok.edu
Phone: (918) 449-6516 37

First published in 2009 by
Business Expert Press, LLC
222 East 46th Street, New York, NY 10017
www.businessexpertpress.com

ISBN-13 (paperback): 978-1-60649-048-8
ISBN-10 (paperback): 1-60649-048-6

ISBN-13 (e-book): 978-1-60649-048-8
ISBN-10 (e-book): 1-60649-048-6

A publication in the Business Expert Press Strategic Management collection

Collection ISSN (print): Forthcoming
Collection ISSN (electronic): Forthcoming

DOI: 10.4128/9781606490495
Cover design by Artistic Group—Monroe, NY
Interior design by Scribe, Inc.

First edition: August 2009

10 9 8 7 6 5 4 3 2 1

Printed in the United States of America.

*For Cecelia and Marquita to whom I hope
to leave the world a better place. —N. E. L.*

*To Jeremy and Jamie for your patience
and understanding throughout my
academic pursuits. —S. D. E.*

Abstract

Sustainable (and green) business seems to have become mainstream practically overnight. This growth in interest in sustainable business practices stems from changing societal expectations and a growing awareness that sustainability creates a win–win situation for the business and humanity alike. *Sustainable Business: An Executive's Primer* is a brief introduction to sustainability as it applies to business. This book will offer an overview of how sustainability is applied throughout the organization. We offer chapters organized by familiar departments or functions of the business and cover the applications and terminology of sustainability throughout each area. Whether you are an executive, an entrepreneur, an employee, or a business student, this book will help you understand the big picture of what it means to be a sustainable business and will give you the information you need to begin your journey toward sustainability.

Keywords

sustainability, sustainable business, green business, strategy, strategic management, climate change, greenhouse gas, carbon emissions

Contents

Acknowledgments

We gratefully acknowledge the feedback and suggestions offered by the following individuals:

Karen Frame	Ciara Spillane	Brigitte Armato
Cynthia Daily, Ph.D.	Dilene Crockett, Ph.D.	Jennifer Powers
Nancy Hopkins	David Wood	Heather Sanders
Lance Lide	Scott Wright	David Dearman, Ph.D.
LaQuinta Broyles	Sherrie Kearney	Thomas Tudor, Ph.D.

PART I

Sustainability Throughout the Organization

CHAPTER 1

Introduction

Going green, green business, and sustainable business are topics on everyone's mind. But what does all this mean exactly? *Sustainable Business: An Executive's Primer* answers that question and provides an introduction to the basics you need to know.

We begin with an understanding of the background of the concept of sustainability and how it applies to the business world. In 1987, the Brundtland Commission put forth a "global agenda for change" with the purpose of "furthering the common understanding and common spirit of responsibility so clearly needed in a divided world."[1] The report outlined the following description of sustainable development:

1. Sustainable development is development that meets the needs of the present without compromising the ability of future generations to meet their own needs. It contains within it two key concepts:

   • the concept of "needs," in particular, the essential needs of the world's poor, to which overriding priority should be given; and
   • the idea of limitations imposed by the state of technology and social organization on the environment's ability to meet present and future needs.

2. Thus the goals of economic and social development must be defined in terms of sustainability in all countries—developed or developing, market-oriented or centrally planned. Interpretations will vary, but they must share certain general features and must flow from a consensus on the basic concept of sustainable development and on a broad strategic framework for achieving it.

3. Development involves a progressive transformation of economy and society.[2]

The concepts of sustainable development and sustainability have since been applied to numerous topics. To understand this definition in terms of business, we will define sustainable business as *one that oper-ates in the interest of all current and future stakeholders in a manner that ensures the long-term health and survival of the business and its associated economic, social, and environmental systems.* Thus a sustainable business is concerned about the current and future social, environmental, and economic impacts associated with its operations. Ideally, the sustainable business seeks to have a positive social impact, a reduced negative envi-ronmental impact, and a positive economic impact (social, environmen-tal, and economic impact will be discussed in further detail in chapter 2). The business that focuses exclusively on reduced negative environmen-tal impact is referred to as a green business, or a business that is "going green." *Sustainable Business: An Executive's Primer* is concerned with the larger picture, or the combined three-dimensional social, environmental, and economic impacts of a sustainable business, that is, the ability of the business to meet present needs while ensuring long-term survival for future generations.

Sustainable (and green) business became mainstream practically over-night; sustainability has transitioned from hippie to hip. This growth in interest in sustainable business practices stems from changing societal expectations and a growing awareness that sustainability creates a win–win situation for the business and humanity alike. The emphasis on sustainable business operations and practices is expected to intensify in the future, particularly given the passage of the American Recovery and Reinvestment Act of 2009, which gives priority to sustainability-related investments in the American economy.

Businesses practicing sustainability improve their image and reputa-tion, reduce costs, and help boost the local economy, all of which lead to improved business and stronger and healthier local communities for operations. Furthermore, these benefits set one company apart from its competitors and can become a source of competitive advantage. This book will provide a rich array of business examples demonstrating a vari-ety of approaches in which businesses seek to maximize social, environ-mental, or economic impacts and any combination of the three in order to become a sustainable business.

The company that seeks to be a sustainable business should under-stand that sustainability is a company-wide goal that incorporates every aspect of the business and its relationships. In other words, sustainability requires systems thinking. Systems thinking is the awareness and understanding that everything is related in some way and that nothing exists in isolation. Every person, every department, every business, every industry, and every society are interrelated and connected in some way. Therefore, it is understood that each part of the business has a contribution to make in helping the company become a sustainable business. That is, the daily operations, research and development, management information systems and information technology, human resources, finance and accounting, and marketing departments are each engaged in sustainability in a different way, yet through *Sustainable Business: An Executive's Primer* you will begin to see the great degree of interconnectedness between each part of the business. Because sustainability is a company-wide philosophy or way of thinking, there will be much coordination required between the various parts of the business and there will ultimately be overlap. The contribution of each area of the business is critical to the overall success of becoming a sustainable business.

Sustainable Business: An Executive's Primer is divided into two sections. Part I is organized along common business functional areas to allow the reader to see how each aspect of the business has a unique contribution to make in helping the business pursue the overarching goal of sustainability. In chapter 2 of this section, we discuss how sustainability is at the heart of company operations. We further explore what the term sustainability means and its emphasis on the triple bottom line. In chapter 3, we show how sustainability is related to the human resources function of the company. We organize the discussion by the components of human resources management: recruitment and selection, training and development, performance appraisal and feedback, and pay and benefits. Our human resources chapter concludes with a discussion on human rights issues. In chapter 4, we discuss how sustainability impacts the function and industry of finance. In the finance function, we review how sustainability considerations play into capital investments and financial investments as well as measures of firm performance. In the finance industry, we discuss how sustainability has generated a new area of finance, carbon finance, and how sustainability impacts the areas of banking and insurance. In chapter 5, we discuss sustainability within the context of the research and development function and show how sustainability is generating new ways of thinking when it comes to research and product design. In chapter 6, we discuss sustainability within the common components of marketing: product, price, place (distribution), and promotion. Chapter 7 discusses how sustainability can help increase efficiency, reduce costs, and track key indicators through information technology and management information systems. Chapter 8 discusses how the accounting function can measure and report its sustainability-related performance. Finally, chapter 9 discusses sustainability as an integral component of the overall strategic direction of the firm.

Part II of the book begins with real case examples of sustainable business practices. We provide very brief examples of over 50 businesses implementing sustainability into their daily operations. Finally, the book concludes with an appendix featuring a list of resources gleaned from each chapter. These resources are the organizations mentioned throughout each chapter to which a business may turn for information, guidance, and assistance on a particular area of expertise.

As you read *Sustainable Business: An Executive's Primer*, we challenge you to not think of sustainability as a program, an initiative, or an activity. Rather, sustainability is a mind-set, a philosophy, and worldview. Throughout each chapter, you are challenged to alter the way you view your job, the workplace, the business, and the world. Whether you are an executive, an entrepreneur, or an employee, *Sustainable Business: An Executive's Primer* will help you understand the big picture of what it means to be a sustainable business and will give you the information you need to begin your journey toward sustainability.

CHAPTER 2

Operations Management

Business operations are at the heart of sustainability. You cannot become a sustainable business without honestly and critically analyzing your current operations and considering the changes necessary to move toward sustainability. In this chapter, we will explain the three dimensions of sustainability and will provide examples of businesses focused on each dimension. In part II of this book, we provide numerous examples of sustainable business practices. The examples here and in part II will demonstrate the variety of ways in which a business can pursue sustainability.

Sustainable Business

Recall from chapter 1 that a sustainable business is one that is concerned about the social, environmental, and economic impacts associated with its current and future operations and the ability of the business to meet present needs while ensuring its and others' long-term survival. Ideally, the sustainable business seeks to have a positive social impact, environmental impact, and economic impact. Taken together, a business's contribution to social justice, environmental quality, and economic prosperity is collectively referred to as the triple bottom line.[1] The triple bottom line (social, environmental, economic) is sometimes referred to as *people, planet, profit.*

Once considered the purview of governments and nonprofit organizations (such as Heifer International, a global leader in developing sustainable communities), businesses are increasingly being called upon to address social, environmental, and economic issues. Rethinking the business in terms of its triple bottom line impact and performance (social, environmental, and economic) is critical in establishing the foundation for sustainable business. This requires a shift away from thinking of a business only in terms of its financial profit to shareholders. While financial profit is necessary for survival, the sustainable business applies a broader view of the business, its responsibilities, and its performance. Therefore,

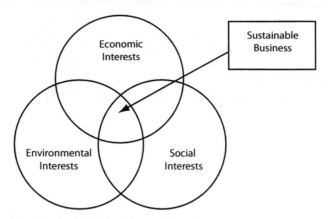

Figure 2.1. Sustainable Business

the sustainability of business is discussed in terms of three interrelated and interconnected dimensions: social, environment, and economic.

Social Impact

The first dimension of a sustainable business is its performance relative to societies and social justice, often referred to as social impact. While there is no easy solution for reducing social costs while improving corporate performance and profitability, social impact should not be overlooked. The social impact of a business's operations is viewed both internally and externally and ensures that the business's entire operations across the supply chain are socially responsible and ethical.

Internally, the social impact of a business often refers to practices related to employees and employment with the business. The sustainable business's social impact would include such items as the business's practices and policies related to working conditions, diversity in hiring, opportunities for advancement for women and minorities, lack of discrimination, and the provision of affordable health care and other necessary benefits. In addition, social impact includes wages, breaks, adherence to employment laws, safety, training, and numerous other specific labor practices. Finally, social impact includes the impact on the local public and social services sector as a result of the business's activities. These are only a sample of the many items considered within the social impact of a business's operations. Many of these internal social impacts are discussed in greater detail in chapter 3.

The sustainable business is not only expected to treat its employees in a responsible manner but also ensure that it is engaged with suppliers that share similar values. That is, a sustainable business is also concerned for the labor practices and working conditions of companies within its supply chain to ensure that the supplies and products it purchases were produced responsibly and ethically. Sustainable businesses will make reasonable efforts to ensure they are not purchasing from suppliers engaged in the use of sweatshops, child labor, or other human rights abuses. In some cases, businesses have worked diligently with suppliers to correct these problems, while in other cases businesses have chosen to change suppliers.

When sourcing products from outside an industrialized country, some sustainable businesses will seek Fair Trade products. Fair Trade certification verifies that living wages were paid to producers and that fair and ethical employment practices were used in the creation of products. Many agricultural goods and handicraft items are Fair Trade certified.

In addition to employment practices, social impact refers to respect of others. This entails the respect of individuals and other businesses encountered locally and around the world. A sustainable business will make reasonable efforts to ensure its policies, practices, products, advertising, logo or mascot, and other aspects of the business are not offensive or disrespectful to clients in the global market. See Table 2.1 for tips on how to increase the social impact of your business.

TOMS Shoes is an example of a company making a commitment to maximize its social impact. In 2006, Blake Mycoskie founded TOMS Shoes with the singular mission of improving the lives of children by providing shoes to those in need. Shoes are produced in Argentina and China following fair labor practices while creating minimal environmental impact. Factories are monitored by TOMS and third-party independent auditors. TOMS Shoes are sold online and in retail locations around the world with the promise that for each pair purchased, TOMS will donate a second pair to a child in need in Argentina, South Africa, and other locations around the world. The public is invited to participate in "shoe drops" around the world and to experience firsthand the social contribution of TOMS Shoes.

Table 2.1. Tips to Increase Your Social Impact

Have you considered where your coffee, chocolate, clothing, or other products come from and the conditions under which they were produced? Social impact is one of the three pillars of a sustainable business, but it can be difficult to define and even more difficult to track and measure.

A sustainable business should consider the social impact of its business operations on employees, those employed throughout the supply chain, and on the community. So how can a business begin to maximize its social impact? Here are some practices that will help create positive social impact:

1.	UN Global Compact: Review the 10 principles of the United Nations Global Compact and abide by them, whether or not the business becomes a signatory.
2.	Buy Fair Trade: Seek out opportunities to purchase Fair Trade products for your business. Fair Trade products ensure that those who produced the product in developing countries were paid a fair wage under humane working conditions. You can purchase Fair Trade clothing, handicrafts, coffee, cocoa, sugar, tea, bananas, honey, cotton, wine, fresh fruit, flowers, and other products.
3.	Company policies and practices: Consider the social impact of your company's policies and practices on employees (such as health care coverage, educational opportunities, and worklife balance).
4.	Philanthropy: Evaluate the impact of your corporate giving programs. Find opportunities that are strategically related to your core business, and focus your philanthropy in those areas, benefiting both the community and the business.
5.	Supply chain: Understand the conditions under which the products and supplies you purchase were produced; work with suppliers to achieve transparency throughout the supply chain; check the Web sites of any of the numerous watchdog organizations (e.g., CorpWatch, Sweatshop Watch, International Labor Rights Forum) to find world regions, specific companies, and industries known for human rights abuses that could be occurring within your supply chain.
6.	Labor: First, make sure your business follows policies and practices that are fair to its labor force; a good place to start is SA8000 and the International Labour Standards; review and understand the standards, whether or not your business seeks certification; support freedom of association, collective bargaining, and nondiscrimination in your own place of business as well as with suppliers; in purchasing, avoid products that were produced using forced and child labor. See Green America's 9 Cool Ways to Avoid Sweatshops, http://www.coopamerica.org/programs/sweatshops/whatyoucando/9coolways.cfm; look for certifications from Fair Trade Federation, Fair Labor Association, Social Accountability International, RugMark, Verite, Worker Rights Consortium, or others that have independently evaluated labor conditions.
7.	Social responsibility: Watch for the 2010 scheduled release of the ISO 26000 standards on social responsibility for companies.

Environmental Impact

The second dimension of a sustainable business is its contribution to preserving environmental quality; commonly referred to as environmental impact. Numerous examples exist of companies reducing environmental costs while simultaneously improving company performance and profitability. The environmental impact of a business's operations is viewed both internally and externally. The business that focuses exclusively on its environmental impact, rather than focusing on the triple bottom line emphasis of a sustainable business, is referred to as a green business.

Internally, the environmental impact of a business often refers to practices related to use of natural resources, waste, toxicity, and pollution. For manufacturing companies, the environmental impact can be large and efforts are generally made to reduce waste, toxicity, and pollution within the manufacturing process. International Organization for Standardization (ISO) 14000 is one example of guidelines for firms on environmental practices and reduced impact.

For service companies, the environmental impact is smaller but should not be overlooked. Consider, for example, the amount of waste the company pays to have removed; chemicals used that eventually find their way into the air, water, or ground (such as cleaning compounds, fertilizers, weed killers, and many others); and pollution created by energy usage, employee commutes, or business travel.

Green building (or remodeling) is a fast growing trend among businesses that wish to be more sustainable. Green building refers to the reduction of environmental impact in the design, construction, and ongoing life of the building. The most frequently utilized standards for green building are the Leadership in Energy and Environmental Design (LEED) of the U.S. Green Building Council.

Recycling programs are often part of a sustainable business's efforts to reduce waste and toxicity. Sustainable companies consider both the purchase of recycled items for office supplies, furniture, and other needs, as well as recycling or donating its own unwanted items. While most companies or offices may already recycle paper, aluminum cans, and plastic bottles, there is little that cannot be recycled today. For example, clever artists and designers make purses and handbags from recycled soda pop tabs, newspapers, tires, potato chip bags, barcodes, candy wrappers, juice pouches, rice bags, and more. As another example of recycling, Caracalla, a salon and day spa in Little Rock, Arkansas, recycles cut hair by sending it to the nonprofit Matter of Trust to be woven into hair mats capable of absorbing chemical oil spills. Many restaurants recycle used grease through companies that purchase "yellow grease." Companies can also recycle office furniture and equipment through donations to charitable giving programs at schools and other nonprofits. Numerous options exist to recycle or donate electronics. If you cannot find a suitable place to recycle or donate your company's unwanted items, consider turning to The Freecycle Network, an online site to give away unwanted items. Many organizations, such as the Zero Waste Alliance, help businesses minimize waste and toxicity. Before discarding anything, the sustainable business will exhaust all possibilities in identifying a second life for the product.

Externally, the sustainable business also considers the environmental impact of suppliers in terms of services and products as well as transportation of goods. A sustainable business will seek out suppliers of services and products that are environmentally friendly. This results in the purchase of products that produce less waste, are less toxic, and generated the least amount of pollution in manufacturing and transportation. Sustainable businesses opt for local suppliers, when possible, in order to reduce the environmental impact caused through the transportation of goods.

Additionally, many sustainable businesses create a green procurement policy, or environmentally preferred purchasing policy, as an integral part of their operations to give preferential purchasing to products and services that are most environmentally friendly. An environmentally preferred purchasing policy would cover all types of products and services purchased by the organization. For example, this policy would give preference to green cleaning products that are less harmful to employees and the environment; or preference to Forest Stewardship Council (FSC) certified wood products that come from sustainably managed forests. As with other attempts to reduce environmental impact, a move toward green procurement can offer cost savings for the sustainable business. For example, Little Rock Athletic Club discovered that if it made the switch to recycled copy paper, the company could achieve a 10% cost savings, 13% fewer carbon dioxide emissions, and 35% fewer trees used when compared to the previous paper products. See Table 2.2 for more tips on how to green your office.

Table 2.2. Tips to Green Your Office
Here are some steps that your office can take to reduce your environmental impact (and save money!):

1.	Use e-mail instead of paper.
2.	Print and copy on both sides of the paper.
3.	Buy recycled paper with the highest percentage of recycled content.
4.	Use environmentally friendly cleaning supplies and detergents.
5.	Purchase refillable office products (cartridges, pens, etc.).
6.	Unplug items not in use or not used frequently.
7.	Switch to a green hosting service for your Web site.
8.	Report and repair water drips and leaks immediately.
9.	Start a vanpool or carpool program.
10.	Create a green team to continue the work toward greening your office or workplace.

There are two additional considerations in determining a company (and supplier's) environmental impact: water efficiency and energy efficiency. When a sustainable business considers water usage—often referred to as a water footprint—it is seeking ways to become more efficient by reducing its use of fresh water or increasing its recycle rate for water. For example, some businesses have collected water from sink, water fountain, shower, dishwasher, and washing machine drains (collectively referred to as greywater systems) or installed rainwater collection systems to recycle water for use in landscaping, decorative water features, and to flush toilets.

When a sustainable business considers energy usage (often referred to as a carbon footprint or energy audit), it is seeking ways to become more efficient and reduce its energy usage. Through an energy audit, many companies have identified sources of wasted energy and accompanying opportunities to become more energy efficient. For example, in the past, landfills often burned off methane generated from decaying waste. Technologies now allow landfills to cap the methane and use it as a renewable energy source.

The generation and consumption of electricity creates emissions of carbon dioxide (CO_2), or carbon emissions. Within industrialized countries, a business emits a significant amount of carbon emissions. CO_2 is one type of greenhouse gas (GHG) that contributes to climate change (for an objective source of scientific information related to climate change, please visit the Web site of the 2007 Nobel Peace Prize winner, Intergovernmental Panel on Climate Change: http://www.ipcc-wg2.org). All other types of greenhouse gases are measured in their CO_2 equivalents; thus reference to carbon is the standard metric. As a result of the large energy usage and subsequently large carbon emissions (or carbon footprints), many businesses are actively engaged in finding ways to reduce carbon emissions by becoming more energy efficient.

The reduction of carbon emissions, or a reduction of the business's carbon footprint, is particularly appealing to businesses today partly because of the possibility of a future carbon tax and the growing carbon trade market (see chapter 4). A carbon tax is enacted and regulated by the government and would add a tax to businesses based on the amount of carbon they emit in their daily operations. A carbon emissions trading system allows businesses to trade "credits" for carbon emissions. Emissions trading, sometimes referred to as a cap-and-trade system, is enacted and regulated by the government, which determines a maximum amount (or cap) of carbon emissions permitted by businesses. Businesses with emissions in excess of the cap will be required to purchase carbon credits (or carbon allowances) from businesses with emissions less than the cap and that have excess carbon credits to sell. There are already several cap-and-trade systems in place.

European Union Emissions Trading Scheme. The European Union has had a mandatory cap-and-trade system since 2005, the European Union Emissions Trading Scheme. It is the largest multinational, multisector system in the world.

New South Wales Greenhouse Gas Reduction Scheme. The New South Wales Greenhouse Gas Reduction Scheme began in 2003 and is a voluntary regional initiative in Australia. The prime minister of Australia will be expanding this system into a mandatory national market by 2010. New mandatory systems are also being considered by leaders in Japan and Canada.

New Zealand Emissions Trading Scheme. The New Zealand Emissions Trading Scheme began in 2009. The scheme is an important component of the country's goal to be carbon neutral by 2020.

Kyoto Protocol. The Kyoto Protocol is a voluntary multinational, multisector cap-and-trade system. According to the cap-and-trade system, companies from 39 Kyoto Protocol participating industrial nations have a cap on the amount of greenhouse gases to be emitted. Companies are issued carbon permits for their portion of the allocated emissions. The system also allows for emissions trading between member countries. Under the Protocol, industrialized nations can earn emissions credits (or carbon credits) for investing in clean technology projects in emerging economies.

In the United States, the only industrialized country in the world that has not ratified the Kyoto Protocol, there is an emerging infrastructure of voluntary cap-and-trade systems and emissions trading markets. These have arisen in response to the growing awareness of the impact of business activities on the environment as well as in anticipation of a forthcoming mandatory system. For example, as part of the solution to global warming, U.S. President Barack Obama supports the creation of a market value in ecosystem sustainability.[2] His plan would put forth a goal to reduce carbon emissions to 80% below 1990 levels by 2050, although there is no current mandatory mechanism in place to support or enforce this goal.

Chicago Climate Exchange. The Chicago Climate Exchange (CCX) is the most well-established North American voluntary cap-and-trade program. Although voluntary, the CCX becomes legally binding and provides third-party independent verification. The CCX also trades carbon futures through the Chicago Climate Futures Exchange.

Regional Greenhouse Gas Initiative. The Regional Greenhouse Gas Initiative (RGGI) is the first regional mandatory system in the United States. The initiative is administered by 10 Northeastern and Mid-Atlantic states to cap emissions and trade carbon permits. Rather than allocating carbon permits to businesses for free, the RGGI held its first auction of permits in September 2008 and raised $39 million to allow the participating states to invest in energy efficiency and renewable energy technologies.[3] RGGI futures are traded on the Chicago Climate Futures Exchange as part of New York Mercantile Exchange's new Green Exchange.

Western Climate Initiative. The Western Climate Initiative is an initiative of several Western states and Canadian provinces. Although this partnership initiative was created in 2007, a cap-and-trade system is being explored but has not yet been implemented.

Midwestern Greenhouse Gas Reduction Accord. The Midwestern Greenhouse Gas Reduction Accord is an initiative of many Midwestern states and the Canadian province of Manitoba. It is a joint agreement established in 2007 to make efforts to reduce greenhouse gas emissions, although no cap-and-trade system is in place.

At this time, reduction of carbon emissions is voluntary in the United States and none of the aforementioned cap-and-trade systems is binding for U.S. businesses. Nonetheless, as mentioned, the possibility of mandatory carbon reductions has led businesses to analyze energy usage and carbon emissions and seek ways to reduce usage and emissions.

The first step to becoming more energy efficient is to conduct an energy audit (of the company's energy usage) or carbon footprint analysis (of the company's full range of operations) to gather baseline data reflecting current energy usage and subsequent carbon emissions from operations. The business can determine the scope of the analysis to be conducted. In a carbon footprint analysis, Scope 1 emissions will measure the direct emissions from energy created on-site through facilities owned by the company. Scope 2 emissions will measure the indirect emissions that result from the company's purchase of off-site energy through facilities it does not own. Scope 3 emissions will measure other indirect emissions from sources the company does not own and which are created through business activities required to keep the physical facility in operation, such as employee and customer commutes. Scope 3 emissions also consider indirect emissions throughout the company's supply chain as a result of the purchase of services and goods required for the business.

The analysis will help the business pinpoint areas in which energy usage and carbon emissions are high. Depending on the scope of the analysis, businesses often find that the carbon footprint is highest in the areas of energy consumption, waste, and travel and transportation. The business will then explore alternatives for reducing energy usage and reducing its carbon emissions. Within the area of energy consumption, companies may invest in energy efficiency improvements or purchase (or generate its own) energy from renewable sources (as detailed below in the discussion of renewable energy projects). Within the area of waste, companies will actively seek ways to reduce their own waste as well as purchase supplies with minimal packaging. Within the area of travel and transportation, the sustainable business will encourage the use of public transportation, telecommuting, ride sharing, flexible work schedules, and fuel-efficient cars for employees. Additional considerations are environmentally friendly alternatives for product and supply transport, such as increased fleet efficiency, the use of second-generation biofuels (or fuel created from waste), and local sourcing to reduce the number of miles products and supplies travel to reach their final destination.

Once the company has explored alternatives for carbon emissions reductions, the company will develop a plan for reducing energy usage and carbon emissions. The carbon reduction strategy (sometimes referred to as a climate change strategy, climate mitigation strategy, or climate abatement strategy) is a detailed plan of measurable specific goals with specific actions that will be taken and deadlines for achievement. Progress is then measured regularly (often annually or biannually) to determine progress toward the goals of reduced energy usage and carbon emissions.

After a business has done all it can to become energy efficient, it often seeks to compensate for the remaining unavoidable carbon emissions it is creating through its operations. This step is important in the plan if the business's goal is to become carbon neutral (sometimes referred to as zero carbon emissions), which is the elimination of all negative environmental impacts from carbon emissions created through the business's operations. To become carbon neutral and achieve zero carbon emissions, a business may purchase carbon offsets equivalent to the amount of greenhouse gases it is emitting through daily operations. Carbon offsets (sometimes called renewable energy certificates or credits [REC], green certificates, green tags, or tradable renewable certificates) are investments in renewable energy projects that would not be possible without the business's investment in the offset project. Renewable energy projects are projects that create energy from sources other than fossil fuels, such as wind, solar, geothermal, methane, kinetic, hydropower, ocean waves, biomass, or other renewable sources. For example, zoos are capturing methane from animal waste and converting it to energy; subway systems are capturing kinetic energy from passengers to generate power; and nightclub dance floors capture kinetic energy to generate power.

Carbon offset projects are not currently regulated; therefore, third-party independent verification of the project should be a part of any investment made in carbon offsets by sustainable businesses. Additionally, the type of project should be carefully scrutinized before purchasing carbon offsets. For example, there is controversy over the value of planting trees as a carbon offset since actual carbon removed from the air is dependent on many factors, such as climate, soil, type of tree, age of tree, survival rate of saplings, and so on. It is worthwhile to read third-party independent research comparing carbon offset projects and companies, such as those provided by Kollmuss and Bowell,[4] Clean Air-Cool Planet,[5] and others. The state of Colorado and the city of San Francisco have both created local carbon offset programs to ensure any business's (or individual's) purchase of carbon offsets goes to fund local projects.

One of the leading examples of corporate environmental impact can be documented through Wal-Mart. In 2005, CEO Lee Scott created a sustainability vision for Wal-Mart and set forth three ambitious goals: to be supplied 100% by renewable energy, to create zero waste, and to sell sustainable products. According to the company's latest progress report, Wal-Mart continues to experiment with the design of stores and its fifth-generation prototype store uses up to 45% less energy than a typical Supercenter.[6] In 2007, the company purchased enough solar power for 22 facilities,[7] and in 2008 the company purchased enough wind power for 360 stores and facilities,[8] both of which will reduce greenhouse gas emissions. The company has achieved a 25% efficiency improvement in its trucking fleet and has recently installed small efficient diesel engines that allow parked truckers to turn off the motor engine and use the smaller engine for heating and cooling. This is expected to save the company $25 million, 100,000 metric tons of carbon emissions, and 10 million gallons of diesel fuel annually.[9] The company is working with its trucking suppliers to manufacture more aerodynamic and fuel-efficient trucks. The company has also introduced a sustainability scorecard in working with product suppliers to make products with less packaging waste. These few examples represent only a fraction of the environmental improvements made by Wal-Mart over the past 4 years. See Table 2.3 for small changes you can make to green your business.

Table 2.3. FREE Ways to Begin Greening Your Business
Here are some tips for the business that wants to start the journey toward green but does not have the funds to implement big changes. All the tips below are free to implement but require a change in behavior away from current practices.

1.	Office paper: Switch from 100% virgin fiber paper products to recycled paper products. For example, we recently compared a business's current office and copier paper purchases to recycled office and copier paper. The final combination of paper choices recommended to the client represented a 10% cost savings, 13% fewer carbon dioxide emissions, and 35% fewer trees used when compared to their previous product. Other recycled paper products to consider are file folders, hanging file folders, notebook pads, binders, calendars, posters, envelopes, business cards, letterhead, forms, self-stick notes, and anything else made from paper! Savings: cost reductions, carbon dioxide emissions reductions (carbon dioxide emissions contribute to climate change), and fewer trees used.
2.	Hand towels: Switch from 100% virgin fiber hand towels to recycled content hand towels. In a recent comparison for a client, we were able to identify 100% recycled hand towels that represented a 2% cost savings over their current product. Savings: cost reductions, carbon dioxide emissions reductions, and fewer trees used.
3.	Toilet tissue: Switch from 100% virgin fiber bath tissue to recycled content bath tissue. In a recent comparison for a client, we were able to identify 100% recycled bath tissue that represented a 46% savings over their current product. Savings: cost reductions, carbon dioxide emissions reductions, and fewer trees used.
4.	Napkins: Switch from 100% virgin fiber napkins to recycled content napkins. In a recent comparison for a client, we were able to identify 100% recycled napkins that represented a 10% cost savings over their current product. Savings: cost reductions, carbon dioxide emissions reductions, and fewer trees used.
5.	Facial tissue: Switch from 100% virgin fiber tissues to recycled content tissues. In a recent comparison for a client, we were able to identify 100% recycled tissues that represented a 4% cost savings over their current product. Savings: cost reductions, carbon dioxide emissions reductions, and fewer trees used.
6.	Lighting: Turn off lights when not in use, and when replacing, use more energy-efficient lighting, such as compact fluorescent bulbs or LED lighting. Savings: can help reduce energy bills.
7.	Electronics and office equipment: Turn off when not in use, and when purchasing, make sure it is ENERGY STAR certified. Dispose of old electronics through a recycling program (most cities will take old electronics for recycling). Old office electronics, furniture, and equipment can also go to donation programs through public schools, Habitat for Humanity ReStore, or other worthy causes. Savings: can help reduce energy bills, can reduce the amount of waste you pay to have removed, and will keep dangerous chemicals out of landfills.
8.	Recycling: Check with your city sanitation department (or check the Earth911 search engine) to see what can be recycled and where it can be recycled. Common items for recycling include aluminum cans, glass, paper, plastic (including plastic bags), cardboard, Styrofoam packaging (Styrofoam food containers are not often recycled), electronics, cooking oil or grease, printer and ink-jet cartridges, and many other items. Savings: can reduce the amount of waste you pay to have removed.
9.	Employee coffee mugs or drink cups: Encourage employees to bring reusable coffee mugs or drink cups (and plates and utensils) rather than using disposables. Savings: can reduce the number of disposable items you purchase and can reduce the amount of waste you pay to have removed.

10.	Office supplies: Use recyclable or refillable items, such as printer cartridges, pens, CD and DVD disks, batteries, and other products. Savings: can help reduce the amount of office items needing replacement and can reduce the amount of waste you pay to have removed.
11.	Printing and copying: For printing, begin by resetting the default font size on all computers to 10 or 11, if feasible, and resetting the default margin to 0.8 or 0.9. By changing the default margin settings to 0.75 on university computers, Penn State found that they could save per year over $122,000 in paper costs, 45,142 reams of paper, 45 tons of waste, and 72 acres of forest. Use your computer and e-mail program as your filing system rather than printing hard copies. Use a printer management software program, such as GreenPrint or PaperCut, that will alert you to wasted paper (such as printing a sheet with one or two lines). Learn to use online forms and PDF files. Next time you send out a printing job, select a green printing company. For copying, change the default settings on the copy machine from one-sided to two-sided copies. By utilizing a combination of suggestions, students at the University of Arkansas at Little Rock found that the College of Business could save 39% or more per year in paper and ink costs. Savings: can reduce the amount of paper you buy, can reduce the amount of waste you pay to have removed, and can reduce your company's carbon emissions.
12.	Cleaning supplies: Use green cleaning products or a green cleaning service. Savings: there may not be any financial savings here, but you are taking steps toward healthier indoor air quality, and your cleaning methods will be releasing fewer toxins into the environment.
13.	Web site: Switch to a green or carbon neutral Web host provider. There are many Web host providers available that are competitively priced. Savings: cost savings and reduced carbon emissions.
14.	Promotional products: Next time you purchase promotional products for your business, select those that are environmentally friendly, are made from recycled material, can be recycled, or those that are all three of these criteria, such as SIGG water bottles. Savings: there may not be any financial savings here, but you are taking steps toward being environmentally friendly and communicating that message to your customers.
15.	Green team: Establish a green team of employees who are interested in helping your business become more environmentally friendly. The green team's focus should be twofold: identifying additional ways to make your business more environmentally friendly and educating employees, customers, and suppliers on the importance of being environmentally friendly as well as communicating the businesss efforts and accomplishments in this arena.

Where do you find these products? You can begin by checking with your current supplier. If your supplier doesn't carry the products, you can check with other local vendors, national suppliers, or online. If you implement the suggestions above, you will begin the journey toward green and will simultaneously save some green!

Source: Barakovic et al. (2009).

Economic Impact

The third dimension of a sustainable business is economic impact. The economic impact of a business's operations is viewed internally and externally. The sustainable business will consider its own economic impact on the communities in which it operates, such as job creation, impact on local wages, impact on real estate in close proximity to the business, tax flows, investment in disadvantaged areas, impact on public works and social services systems, and other indicators that the business has positively contributed to local economic growth while maintaining corporate profitability. Economic impact does not refer to the profitability of the business as indicated on the financial statements, although profitability is critical for survival. The sustainable business will also look externally at suppliers to ensure they are engaged across the supply chain with other companies that share similar values and practices. It is assumed that the sustainable business's contribution to a strong and healthy local economy will lead to a strong and healthy future for the business.

The El Dorado Promise, a strategic philanthropy initiative of Murphy Oil Corporation, is an inspired example of corporate economic impact.[10] Murphy Oil Corporation, a Fortune 500 company, is headquartered in El Dorado, Arkansas, a small, rural township with an estimated population of 20,341.[11] In order to address the interrelated problems of declining industry, population, school enrollment, and talent pool from which to draw, Murphy Oil Corporation announced that it would donate $50 million to a scholarship program for local students, creating the El Dorado Promise program. The program is expected to provide scholarships to students for the next 20 years.

One year after announcing the Promise program, there was an 18% increase in college-bound seniors.[12] After 2 years, the community has seen a 4% increase in school enrollment, the local community college has seen a 16% increase in enrollment, and families from more than 28 states and 10 foreign countries have moved to El Dorado.[13]

The inspiring examples of TOMS Shoes, Wal-Mart, and Murphy Oil Corporation demonstrate the significant impact a company can have in pursuing any of the dimensions of sustainable business. In each of these examples, we see how the social, environmental, or economic commitment has become central to the way in which the business conducts its operations. In part II of this book, we provide an array of additional examples that we hope will inspire your own business to begin its journey toward sustainability.

CHAPTER 3

Human Resources

Integrated, innovative human resource practices are essential in creating a corporate culture that ensures sustainability is valued and maintained at all levels of the organization. Such practices have the ability to generate a significant social, environmental, and economic impact. To achieve a competitive advantage in business, it is imperative for organizations to place high priority on their internal human capital. Chapter 3 examines human resource issues in recruitment and selection, training and development, performance appraisal and feedback, pay and benefits, and labor relations.

Recruitment and Selection

The sustainable organization will be a community employer whenever possible. Recruitment and selection generates a social and economic impact on the community. Corporations want to find qualified workers and many times will use national recruiting agencies. Bringing in new employees from outside the community can provide a social benefit by increasing the number of residents for the community, which, in turn, increases spending in the community, housing starts, improvements in infrastructure, and growth of programs. On the other hand, hiring within the community decreases unemployment numbers and sustains the social and economic quality of life. Employment not only creates a means by which to live, but it also increases skills within the area that develops a stable labor pool for hiring. Sustainable companies should act as a community employer; they can be socially responsible to current employees by filling upward mobility positions internally and promoting from within whenever possible.

Recruiting tools such as Web sites, videos, presentations, and literature should include the company's philosophy on sustainability. In particular, recruiters need to make the company's environmental stance a priority in promoting the firm to potential applicants. In the advertisement, bring attention to any successful environmental endeavors or any awards won for environmentalism. However, it is important that recruiters not inflate environmental claims of the company, which is termed greenwashing (to be discussed further in chapter 6).

In addition to traditional recruitment outlets, choose magazines or trade journals whose audience is open to sustainability issues. There are several print and online sites focused on the recruitment of individuals seeking employment with a sustainable business (see Table 3.1). These specialty recruitment services bring together sustainable companies with sustainability-minded potential employees.

The availability and use of online recruiting and online application submissions are increasing in firms that have sustainability as a core value in order to save on printed materials and mailings. However, if printing is necessary, brochures and other recruiting literature should use recycled stock with soy-based inks and include that fact on the document itself.

The firm's selection criteria should be aligned with sustainability criteria. A thorough needs assessment and job analysis will provide insight into the knowledge, skills, and abilities that will facilitate accomplishment of sustainability. The best candidates for employment will have a

Table 3.1. Sustainability Recruitment
There are a number of print and online media outlets for the recruitment of employees for the sustainable business.

Acre
Business for Social Responsibility
Corporate Responsibility Officer
CSRwire
Ethical Corporation
GreenBiz
Green Dream Jobs
Idealist
Net Impact
Stopdodo
Sustainable Industries

propensity toward sustainable views and will indicate an "organizational fit" for the company and its goals. Job descriptions will reflect appropriate requirements for jobs that require a more substantial knowledge of sustainability such as purchasing, marketing, and fleet management, to name a few. Interviewing can also be made more environmentally friendly. Several Web sites, such as GreenJobInterview.com,[1] have been developed to assist in conducting synchronous or asynchronous virtual interviews with candidates that can reduce transportation costs and associated carbon emissions.

The sustainable firm is definitely an equal opportunity employer. The principle of fair and equal treatment is an integral part of sustainability endeavors. Selection tests and interviews will avoid unfair or discriminatory questions and requirements. Companies are putting focus on diversity because it plays an important role in the reputation of the firm, in decision making, in relationships with suppliers and other stakeholders, and in the hiring processes. The advantage comes from the diversity of ideas and values that stimulate innovation. Women and minorities have been projected to enter the workforce in increasing quantities in the future. A company runs the risk of missing high quality employees if equal opportunities in the company are deficient.

Training and Development

New employees must be oriented to the company's stance on sustainability issues and what the expectations are for the employee to further sustainability efforts. The company, however, will continue to conduct sustainability training for all employees at all levels, including management. Sustainability curricula have been developed by the nonprofit organization Northwest Earth Institute and are appropriate for workplace training.

Companies have historically provided ethics, diversity, and leadership training, but sustainability education and training must reorient the way employees view their jobs and the business. Employees should ultimately be trained to rethink every aspect of the job and workplace in terms of sustainability: relationships between systems; long-term survival and quality of life for social, economic, and environmental systems; reduced waste, pollution, and toxicity; increased efficiencies; increased harmony of the person and business with other social, economic, and environmental systems; and innovative ways to reduce, reuse, and recycle. Increasing employee awareness fosters creative solutions to business problems through a sustainability lens.

In addition to general training to help employees understand sustainability concepts, employees can be taught sustainability-related skills specific to the job function. This might include triple bottom line accounting, carbon accounting, social accounting, carbon finance, life cycle analysis, life cycle costing, benchmarking, and other sustainability-related skills relevant to job duties (each of which we discuss within the relevant chapters).

Sustainable organizations can create green training facilities and conduct green meetings. In particular, meeting rooms should be energy efficient by using energy efficient lighting, motion detectors for lighting, and ENERGY STAR computers and equipment. Companies can seek to minimize the number of handouts or papers, use only recycled paper, and reduce and recycle waste. If food is served, the organization should use vendors that supply organic food grown or raised locally. If your company will conduct meetings at hotels or other companies' facilities, make sure the supplier provides green meeting facilities and services. When hiring others to provide training, incorporate sustainability requirements as part of the standard request for proposals.

Training can be conducted either on the job or off the job. Businesses focusing on sustainability are increasingly conducting more on-the-job training and engaging in travel reduction programs. Virtual conferences are growing in popularity due to their reduced economic and environmental impact. In addition, video conferencing is growing in popularity for the same reasons. For example, Vodafone, a telecommunications company, uses video conferencing in order to reduce company-wide travel. It is estimated that the use of video conferences eliminates 13,500 flights per year and 5,500 tons of carbon emissions for the company.[2] Within one year, the dollars saved under this initiative provided a return on the investment.[3] Products, such as GoToMeeting.com,[4] are available to facilitate Web conferencing and virtual meetings.

E-learning, virtual classrooms, and computer- or Web-based learning environments have many advantages. These options allow trainees to perform at their own pace, they offer multimedia capabilities, they save costs, and they can standardize learning across locations. These forms of training are an efficient way to deliver learning content, and the organization can track employee training performance through scores and completions. Again, these forms of training will reduce travel and associated economic and environmental costs.

Companies are increasingly using Webinars, or seminars on the Web, for training. Due to the popularity of Webinars offered by third-party trainers, there are often many from which to choose (both free and paid). In a live Webinar, there are typically a small number of participants, which allows for more interaction and involvement. In many cases, live Webinars are archived on the Internet for later viewing. Companies can also use GoToWebinar.com[5] to host their own Webinar.

Particularly effective training tools are simulations, or situations that replicate job demands. Several industries, such as airline, health care, emergency services, and law enforcement, have frequently utilized simulations. This has resulted in cost savings associated with equipment and travel and a reduction in accident rates.[6] Sustainable organizations that engage in off-the-job training should contract specifically with those that can make claims to being green service providers.

In addition to company-sponsored training and development opportunities, sustainable businesses recognize the need to allow employees to develop to their fullest potential and to flourish in their own personal development. This requires respecting the employee's need for personal growth, development, and fulfillment and allowing reasonable opportunity to pursue those needs. Some companies accept spirituality in the workplace; others allow ample time for community service and involvement (whether paid or unpaid by the company). Other companies may encourage employees to use their job-related skills for professional service through a variety of nonprofit organizations (see Table 3.2).

Lastly, beyond training employees for a specific company's needs, there exists a worldwide shortage of potential employees with the proper skills to further the development of a green economy and the ability to do business in a carbon-constrained world.[7] Several surveys reveal that a shortage of trained workers, from technical to professional, is the primary roadblock to the development of a green economy. Job training programs,

Table 3.2. Use Your Business Skills to Make a Difference
There are a number of nonprofit organizations that seek out business persons to donate their valuable professional skills:

Business Council for Peace
CEOs Without Borders
Diplomats Without Borders
Financial Services Volunteer Corp
Geekcorps
International Executive Service Corps
MBA-Nonprofit Connection
MBAs Without Borders
Net Impact
New Ventures
Taproot Foundation
TeamMBA
TechnoServ
Wall Street Without Walls

colleges, and universities are beginning to recognize this deficit and create training and education programs to help develop a green workforce. In addition, professional organizations, such as the International Sustainability Professionals Society, are beginning to emerge.

Green-collar jobs refer to the modification of blue-collar jobs by incorporating new environmentally related knowledge, skills, and abilities into positions that will aid in the transition to a green economy. The demand for green-collar, technical, and professional workers is expected to continue experiencing rapid growth and increasing demand.[8] As proof, the renewable energy industry grew more than 3 times as fast as the U.S. economy in 2007 and renewable energy and energy efficiency are expected to generate millions of jobs for both professional and technical workers.[9] Extensive information on green-collar jobs can be obtained from the nonprofit organizations Green For All and Apollo Alliance.

Performance Appraisal and Feedback

Most companies engage in the traditional performance appraisal system where the employee's performance is measured on some prescribed criteria. The purpose of performance appraisals is generally to provide feedback to the employee on his or her performance in order to correct any deficiencies and to create increased opportunities. Employees are not always satisfied with the performance appraisal process. However, some form of assessment is needed to provide feedback for improvement. Recognition of performance levels can serve to motivate workers toward higher levels of performance or more creative solutions to problems.

Some companies have tied performance appraisals to sustainability performance. Identification of performance dimensions is an important first step in the process. Performance criteria should be directly tied to business goals and objectives. Measures should be meaningful and controllable. Since one of the sustainable organization's goals is to pursue triple bottom line performance, performance appraisal dimensions should reflect the importance of sustainability in the criteria. Management can weight the various economic, social, and environmental criteria higher than other criteria in order to indicate the importance of sustainability to the employee. Performance management should hold managers accountable for meeting sustainability goals through employees.

Trait, behavioral, and outcome appraisal instruments can be altered to include sustainability criteria. Trait appraisal instruments ask the supervisor to make judgments about characteristics of the employee. Typical traits are reliability, energy, loyalty, and decisiveness. Organizations can add traits such as efficient, honesty, or communicative to depict traits the company would like to see employees exhibit. Behavioral appraisal instruments are developed to assess workers' behaviors, such as ability to work well with others, promptness, and development of personal skills. Sustainable examples might be working toward reducing waste or consciously using techniques that reduce negative social impacts. Finally, outcome appraisal instruments assess results. In addition to total sales or number of products produced, sustainable companies can assess energy usage, amount of miles saved on transportation, or recycling levels.

In line with other areas of human resources that suggest online or Web applications, performance appraisals are no different. Organizations can use Web-based performance appraisal software, such as Halogen eAppraisal[10] or EmpXtrack,[11] to prevent excess use of paper products and to increase transparency of the process.

Essential to the success of performance appraisal systems on sustainable performance is the cooperation and approval of the employees. The employee must feel that the assessment process will lead to the improvement of the overall sustainability of the company. The need for employee buy-in may require the company to engage in capacity-building activities. One consulting firm suggests capacity-building activities such as providing access to various databases, libraries, or Web sites; creating publications; conducting training; providing consultation; coordinating alliances; and implementing team-building tasks.[12]

Pay and Benefits

Pay and benefits policies promoted by the organization will have a great social and economic impact on employees and communities. For example, company policies and practices can transfer the burden to and add stress on local social services systems as a result of inadequate wages and benefits.

The sustainable organization would benefit from ensuring the compensation structure is fair and equitable. Fair pay can be viewed internally and externally to the organization. Internal equity exists when the employees generally perceive fairness in the pay structure across employees. External equity refers to the perceived fairness of pay relative to what other employers are paying for similar labor. The ability to ensure the fairness of compensation is a difficult task. Sustainable companies want to attract the best employees by paying above-market compensation yet remain fair to existing employees with tenure. The organization should conduct pay studies annually to ensure programs remain competitive and implement an annual review cycle for ongoing monitoring. Managers can access salary data through online compensation surveys, such as those available at HR.com,[13] Salary.com,[14] or SalarySource.com,[15] which provide information by location, industry, position, and work experience.

Companies have a choice to develop compensation systems based upon an elitist system (that which establishes different compensation plans for different employee groups) or an egalitarian system (having most employees under the same equal compensation plan). An egalitarian system is beneficial to highly competitive environments where companies are innovative, risk-taking, and continuously investing in new technologies and projects, which is typically how sustainable companies work. This type of compensation system provides more flexibility in employment by creating fewer differences between employee grades, creating a flatter organizational chart, and minimizing status-dependent perquisites. Fewer differences in compensation plans should result in increased task accomplishment and cooperation among employees by reducing barriers.

Transparency is a cornerstone of the sustainability movement. Even though companies can be transparent in accounting and financial reporting, transparency can also be achieved by communicating openly about policies and practices related to compensation and employment practices. When compensation practices are hidden from employees, they tend to perceive more underpayment than is actually real. Employees tend to compare their pay and benefits to other employees and may inflate any discrepancies they believe they see, thereby causing more dissatisfaction, less productivity, increased absenteeism, and turnover. Transparent compensation plans make management more fair in administering the compensation.

Sustainable organizations should also ensure they pay living wages rather than minimum wages. Minimum wage is set by legislation to be a minimum dollar amount per hour that must be paid by law. By contrast, living wage is the minimum income necessary for a person to attain a specified quality of life given the location and other economic factors where the person is employed. Living wages are generally higher than minimum legal wages. Sustainable firms will recognize the value of living wages in maintaining a productive and sustainable workforce.

In addition to providing living wages, sustainable businesses provide important benefits necessary for employee quality of life. Standard benefits packages, such as health insurance, dental insurance, and paid sick leave, are supplemented with additional benefits addressing work–family balance. Employees are considered to be more satisfied and productive with increased quality of work and home and community life. Sustainable organizations tend to establish work initiatives such as child care centers at the job, time off (leave) from work to care for sick children or elderly family members, paternity leave for male employees, flextime work, telecommuting, job sharing, tax breaks for commuting, and other employee-friendly benefits.

An example of a green employee benefit is demonstrated through HEAL Arkansas, a program started at the Addison Shoe Factory in rural Arkansas. After realizing that many employees spent up to 50% of their income on energy bills, the company implemented an energy-efficiency employee benefit that could help reduce energy bills, increase disposable income, increase quality of life for its employees, and even improve employee retention rates. HEAL Arkansas provides low-cost loans to employees for energy-efficiency home improvements. Employees receive home energy audits with recommendations on how to improve home energy efficiency. Loans are repaid through payroll deduction, which is offset by the employee's energy bill savings.

One specific employee benefit of interest to the sustainable business is the commuter-choice tax benefit. The federal tax code (IRS, section 132f) allows employers to provide commuter-choice tax benefits to employees. Employees who commute to work through transit or car/vanpool can set aside up to $230 per month in pre-tax dollars for commuting expenses and up to $230 per month in pre-tax dollars for parking expenses. The employer can then also claim a tax deduction for the expense. Because the value of the benefits paid to employees is listed as a fringe benefit and not listed as wage or salary, the cost of the benefit is therefore considered a business expense and payroll taxes do not apply.

Another example of transportation benefits can be found at Clif Bar and Company, an organic food company in Berkley, California. The company distributes points to employees for selecting alternate modes of transportation to work, such as walking, biking, carpooling, or mass transit. The employees are then able to redeem those points for gift cards, company merchandise, coffee shop items, public transportation passes, or carbon offsets from various organizations that spend the money on projects such as reforestation, renewable energy research, or energy-efficiency technology. Clif Bar and Google, among other companies, actually provide employees an incentive to purchase green vehicles. Clif Bar will provide up to $5,000 to an employee for the purchase of a qualified car; the loan is provided up front and written off at $1,000 per year.[16]

An imperative for a sustainable organization's human resource department is flexibility. One strategy would be to hire contingent workers—employees hired to deal with temporary increases in workload or to complete work that is not part of the core requirements. Contingent workers are generally the first to be dismissed when an organization experiences a downturn. On the one hand, contingent employees provide protection for the full-time employee who might otherwise have been laid off during the downturn. On the other hand, the use of contingent workers ultimately creates a negative social impact. Contingent employees experience uncertainty about their work future, which can affect work performance. An additional human resource for hire would be interns, which would provide a positive social impact for both the individual and the company.

More sustainable ways to provide human resource flexibility can be accomplished through flexible work scheduling such as flexible work hours, compressed workweeks, or telecommuting. Flexible work scheduling can be accomplished through flexible work hours (flextime) where employees can choose to organize work routines that fit with their personal activities and lifestyles as opposed to the traditional workday hours. Compressed workweeks change the number of workdays per week by increasing the length of the workday, which, in turn, reduces the number of days required in a typical workweek. Compressed workweeks have the potential to positively impact the work–life balance and reduce stress for employees by providing extra time for families and activities. When implemented effectively, compressed workweeks have the potential to lower employee absenteeism and turnover rates for organizations. To date, several city, county, and state governments as well as numerous companies have implemented 4-day workweeks for employees with the anticipation of decreased energy and transportation costs and increased employee satisfaction and retention.

Telecommuting provides flexibility in both the hours and the location of work. Employees spend at least one day a month or more working from home while maintaining their connection to the office by phone, fax, and computer. Many employees, particularly highly extroverted individuals, may be more productive when they remove themselves from multiple distractions. Related to telecommuting is a practice called "office hoteling" or "hot desking." Office hoteling is the creation of a software reservation program that reserves office space to employees on an as-needed basis rather than in the manner of the traditional, permanent office space setup. Hot desking involves providing a desk that is shared between several people at different scheduled times. These practices reduce the amount of physical space, which lowers overhead cost and prevents resource hoarding or the underutilization of resources. From an environmental perspective, these methods result in reduced traffic and pollution as well as reduced energy consumption and costs for the company.

Labor Relations

Labor relations refer to the interaction between the company and the employee, particularly related to the employee's right to organize. A sustainable company will take a broader view of labor relations and interpret the term to include the protection of labor and human rights with regard to the impacts of business.

Operating within the law has benefits beyond simple legal compliance. A sustainable organization does so because it believes it is the right thing to do for the welfare of the organization and its employees. The human resources department has a large responsibility to keep records, maintain policies, and monitor actions to ensure that employee human rights are protected. Multinational companies operating in emerging economies are especially vulnerable to pressures to exploit the laws, or lack thereof, in other countries. Sustainable organizations practice good citizenship and high ethical standards because it is the right thing to do.

The International Labour Organization has put forth the International Labour Rights Standards by which member states are expected to abide. In addition, there are numerous nonprofit organizations tracking and reporting on working conditions and human rights issues around the world, including Global Exchange, Human Rights Watch, International Labor Rights Forum, and Sweatshop Watch.

A sustainable organization promotes diversity and nondiscrimination. Employee diversity can improve the effectiveness and efficiency of an organization by stimulating greater creativity and improving problem solving. In an organization that values a broader, fuller array of experiences, cultural viewpoints, and values, there is greater potential for more creativity in ideas and problem solving. Practices that promote increased diversity are top management commitment to valuing diversity, diversity training programs, support groups, accommodation of family needs, senior mentoring and apprentice programs, and diversity audits. Support groups can be established by an employer to provide a supportive climate for employees around basic interests or common ground. For example, American Express provides employee-sponsored networks for various groups such as the Jewish Employee Network, the Employees Over the Age of 40 Network, and the Native American Employee Network.[17] The company 3M also provides a Women's Leadership Network, Executive Mentoring Program, and the Disability Advisory Group. Companies, such as Marriott and Honeywell, encourage senior mentoring programs in which senior managers select minority employees to help with career decisions and progress. Even though the networks are employee-sponsored, companies such as Darden Restaurants[18] motivate the networks to be involved in the goals of the business. They require each network to develop a 3-year business plan to show how the network is meeting business goals. They have in place a compensation program for the network's leaders.

A sustainable organization ensures occupational health and safety. Health and safety issues can be viewed in terms of both social and economic impacts. Employees who are protected from hazardous conditions will have a higher quality of life. Additionally, the cost to employers of workers compensation insurance is directly linked to the number of accidents. Employers pay increased premiums when safety records reflect negative results. Organizations will spend less in the long run by implementing programs to ensure good practices. Even the announcement of a penalty can have a significant negative effect on the stock price of a company. Concern for the health and safety of employees should begin with top management, and subsequent levels of management should be tasked with developing awareness and implementing training while being rewarded for health and safety initiatives.

The sustainable organization protects employees from harassment and oppressive work environments. Quid pro quo sexual harassment occurs when sexual activity is requested in return for job benefits.

Hostile work environments occur when an employee perceives the behavior of another as offensive and undesirable. Policies for handling harassment charges should be developed, and managers and employees should undergo training.

The sustainable organization maintains good citizenship behaviors and consistent standards of ethics in international environments. Different cultures may have very different views and laws of what is right and wrong. Companies need to avoid exploitation of laws found in other countries, such as child labor laws, which are common in many developing nations. In the short run, companies may experience competitive disadvantages compared to local firms that are able to utilize child labor in order to lower costs or that are able to utilize excessive overtime (often uncompensated) to increase productivity. However, in the long run, maintaining ethical practices creates goodwill opportunities both domestically and abroad with investors, suppliers, and customers. For further discussion, see the information on base of the pyramid strategies in chapter 9.

This chapter demonstrates the importance of considering social, economic, and environmental impacts within the human resources function. Our discussion here has detailed ways in which human resources managers and companies can improve social impact, improve economic impact, and reduce environmental impacts through the activities associated with recruitment and selection, training and development, performance appraisal and feedback, pay and benefits, and labor relations.

CHAPTER 4

Finance

Julia S. Kwok*

The intersection of sustainability and finance occurs on many fronts. In this chapter, we will discuss how sustainability impacts various activities associated with the finance function, such as investments, banking, trading, insurance, and more. The chapter starts with capital investments, which are long-term corporate finance decisions related to fixed assets and capital structure. The discussion of the valuation techniques centers on the inclusion of sustainability measures in the analysis. Green and socially responsible investment opportunities, such as green bonds and emissions trading, are explored in the financial investment section. We then turn to financial services, such as banking and insurance.

Capital Investments

Prior to the acceptance of sustainable projects, socially responsible organizations have to evaluate the feasibility and sustainability of capital investments. Common financial methods historically employed in capital budgeting decisions include return on investment, payback period, unit cost of service, cost–benefit ratio, internal rate of return, and net present value. However, these methods are not always the best choices in sustainable finance since these methods do not explicitly account for cash flows associated with social, environmental, and economic impacts. These methods tend to externalize rather than internalize sustainable costs imposed on the society.

---

*By Julia S. Kwok, Northeastern State University, 3100 E. New Orleans Street, Department of Accounting and Finance, College of Business and Technology, Broken Arrow, OK 74014. E-mail: kwok@nsuok.edu; Phone: 918-449-6516.

Sustainability Valuation

Valuation determines a company's worth. Sustainability valuation shows how sustainability adds value to the business. Currently, no existing methodology is considered adequate for sustainability valuation. This has led to much debate surrounding the best way to measure sustainability valuation within the firm. A recent McKinsey & Company survey shows that executives believe that improvements in social, environmental, and governance performance create value; however, they do not agree on how much or how to measure it.[1] Naturally, respondents agree that it would be helpful if companies reporting on sustainability performance would quantify financial impact, measure business opportunities as well as risks, and be transparent about methodology.[2]

Research has shown that nonfinancial measures are the leading indicators of a firm's future financial performance.[3] Additionally, research shows that firms listed on the Dow Jones Sustainability Index consistently outperform firms not listed on the Index. Thus, determining appropriate sustainability valuation metrics is particularly critical in this time of increasing emphasis on sustainability.

Given the importance of sustainability valuation but the lack of standardized approaches, several efforts have been made to identify or develop appropriate valuation metrics. In a recent effort to valuate sustainability performance, qualitative reports of progress were analyzed and converted to five common financial metrics: ratio analysis, discounted cash flow analysis, rules of thumb valuation, economic value-added analysis, and option pricing.[4] Other traditional financial approaches used include cost–benefit ratios and net present value.

Yet it is commonly agreed that existing financial metrics are insufficient to capture the real value of sustainability. As a result, a number of new approaches and methods have been proposed: deliberative monetary valuation, social multicriteria evaluation, three-stage multicriteria analysis, multicriteria mapping, deliberative mapping, and stakeholder decision/ dialogue analysis.[5] Yet another approach, the Financial Valuation Tool for Sustainability Investments,[6] has been developed specifically for the extractive industries (mining, gas and oil exploration, etc.) and could serve as an example for other industries. Until appropriate methods are developed and widely adopted, businesses are left to use common financial metrics.

Capital Budgeting Investment

Capital budgeting decisions allow companies to use financial metrics to compare and prioritize investments in sustainability projects. Return on investment, payback period, and unit cost of service can be utilized in cases that have explicit costs and revenues related to sustainable investment. The use of basic capital budgeting tools, such as internal rate of return, net present value, and cost–benefit ratio, will require some adjustments and cautious use in order to accommodate sustainability analysis. Total cost accounting and life cycle costing analysis are excellent tools for a comprehensive analysis of sustainability-related investments (see chapter 8 for a full discussion).

Once capital budgeting projects are analyzed, selected, and prioritized, there may exist various outside financing options for sustainability-related projects. The Database of State Incentives for Renewables and Efficiency (DSIRE)[7] is a good starting point. State and federal regulations related to renewable energy have resulted in state and federal rebates, performance-based incentives, tax credits, tax incentives, power-purchasing agreements, revolving loan funds, and grants. Among some of the incentives you may find at the DSIRE Web site are tax rebates of up to $350,000 per entity to governmental agencies that purchase alternative fuel vehicles for business and official activities. Manufacturers of vehicles designed to operate on alternative fuels or hybrid diesel/electric may get financing assistance from the Alternative Fuels Conversion Program (AFCP). The AFCP will generally fund up to 50% of the additional cost of purchasing hybrid diesel or electric vehicles instead of a regular vehicle. As a result of the American Recovery and Reinvestment Act of 2009, additional sources of financing for investments in sustainability projects will become available.

Another option is performance contracting. Performance contracting is considered a remodeling or construction financing method whereby the business does not pay up front for energy efficiency projects to be integrated into the current project budget but rather finances projects through guaranteed energy savings expected in the future.

Socially Responsible Investments

Socially responsible investing (SRI) refers to the evaluation of investment options in light of its social, economical, and environmental impacts on the globe in the future. This is an ethical investment strategy that focuses on maximizing both an investor's financial return and an investment's sustainability impact. Green investing refers to the investment in securities that focus solely on financing to environmentally conscious businesses.

The Social Investment Forum (SIF) and other SRI publications provide good sources of information about social investing. SIF is a national nonprofit trade association that provides programs and resources to its members to assist them with integrating social, economic, environmental, and governance factors into their investment decisions. The European nonprofit Ethical Investment Research Service also provides a source of research on the social, environmental, and economic performance of various companies as does the Investor Responsibility Research Center and the Sustainable Investment Research International network. Other sources for consumer SRI education can also be obtained from the GreenMoney Journal[8] and Clear Profit Publishing.[9] Both organizations promote SRI and corporate social responsibility through news and research.

SRI is estimated to be a $2.7 trillion industry in the United States.[10] The Interfaith Center of Corporate Responsibility represents the largest association of faith-based institutions making socially responsible investments. Common screens or criteria used to eliminate companies for SRI investments are animal testing, product and worker safety, industry focus (such as gambling, mining, or weapons systems), and product focus (such as alcohol or tobacco).

The proliferation of SRI products and services, such as mutual funds, equity indexes, and investments in individual stocks and bonds, is a reflection of the growing trend in SRI.

Mutual Funds

As a $200 billion business, SRI-focused mutual funds perform competitively with non-SRI funds over time despite concerns for the higher risk levels.[11] Some of the largest families of socially responsible mutual funds are managed by AHA, Calvert, Domini, MMA Praxis, Parnassus, and Pax

World. Selection of companies for these funds are generally screened based on governance, ethics, diversity and women, indigenous people's rights, transparency, equitable and affordable access to water, climate change, stakeholder engagement, weaponry, nuclear power, and other factors.

SRI Indexes

The risk of investing in SRI indexes is lower than investing in individual socially responsible investments. The proliferation of SRI indexes is a reflection of the growing trend for sustainable investment.

Dow Jones Sustainability Indexes (DJSI). The DJSI are comprised of global, European, Eurozone, North American, and U.S. benchmarks. Launched in 1999, DJSI are the first global index tracking the financial performance of leading sustainability companies. The companies are screened based on environmental attributes (climate change strategies, energy consumption), social attributes (human resources development, knowledge management, stakeholder relations), and economic attributes (corporate governance, risk management) in 57 industry sectors.

KLD Indexes. KLD Research & Analytics has developed 19 socially or environmentally related domestic and global indexes.[12] KLD's Domini 400 Social Index was the first benchmark index based on environmental, social, and governance (ESG) factors and has been in use since 1990. It is a value-weighted stock index of 400 publicly traded American companies that are screened based on rankings in employee and human relations, product safety, environmental safety, and corporate governance. The index includes companies not in the S&P 500.

KLD's Global Sustainability Index (GSI) is a broadly diversified global benchmark based on ESG rankings. The GSI lists companies with the highest sustainability rankings. The ranking takes into consideration the environment, community and society, employees and supply chain customers, and governance and ethics. The index tries to limit the financial risk associated with sector bias.

FTSE4Good Index. The FTSE4Good Index Series measures the performance of companies that meet FTSE's globally recognized corporate responsibility standards on their environmental record, development of positive relationships with their stakeholders, and support for universal human rights. Member companies are primarily from the United Kingdom, United States, and Japan.

Opportunities for the Majority (OM) Index. The OM Index represents publicly traded firms operating in base of the pyramid markets (see chapter 9) in Latin America and the Caribbean.

Australian Sam Sustainability Index (AuSSI). The AuSSI was launched in Australia in 2005. The AuSSI represents sustainability leaders in 21 industry clusters.

Green Investment

Green investing refers to the investment in organizations that are committed to environmentally conscious business practices, such as the conservation of natural resources, the production and discovery of alternative energy sources, and the implementation of clean air and water projects.

Despite the fact that investing in green companies is riskier than other investment vehicles due to the life cycle of the companies, 64% of respondents identified the environment as the most desirable investment opportunity.[13] Green bonds, carbon trading, and renewable energy credits (REC) are notable examples of green investments.

Green Bonds, or Qualified Green Building and Sustainable Design Project Bonds, are tax-exempt bonds issued by federal or municipal qualified agencies to businesses to provide financing for green design, green buildings, investment in other projects intended to mitigate climate change, as well as for the development of brownfield sites (underdeveloped or abandoned areas often containing trace amounts of industrial pollution).

Measuring Corporate Performance

As we discuss capital investments and socially responsible investments, it is appropriate that we discuss how to measure corporate performance. Whereas businesses have traditionally assessed corporate performance through financial measures, there is growing emphasis to adopt a long-range and broader perspective that includes nonfinancial measures. There is much support for adopting more comprehensive strategic corporate performance measurement systems. Research has shown that nonfinancial measures are often the leading indicators that drive lagging financial performance.[14] Furthermore, nonfinancial indicators can provide a link between current activities and future financial performance of the firm.[15] Indeed, a triple bottom line orientation requires the inclusion of nonfinancial indicators of company performance.

The balanced scorecard[16] is the most popular performance measurement system currently used that incorporates both financial and nonfinancial measures in evaluating overall firm performance. The most recent biennial survey of management tool usage among corporations worldwide shows that 66% of respondents report their company uses the balanced scorecard.[17] The balanced scorecard provides a comprehensive measure of corporate performance.

The balanced scorecard is comprised of four categories of indicators in the areas of innovation, learning and growth, internal business processes, customer value, and financial performance. Organizations select unique indicators within each area that are directly linked to the organization's strategic goals. Indicators often selected include employee training and corporate culture attitudes, internal business processes, customer requirement conformance and satisfaction, and risk assessment and cost–benefit data. As a management system, it helps identify measures to be taken by providing feedback concerning external outcomes related to internal processes. This allows for the alignment of daily business activities with long-term organizational goals and performance.

There has been an effort by some researchers to show how the balanced scorecard can be used for the sustainability-focused organization.[18] Balanced scorecards that incorporate sustainability considerations are referred to as Sustainability Balanced Scorecards.

Carbon Finance

In general, carbon finance refers to applying a financial management system, models, and tools to manage a company's carbon dioxide and other greenhouse gas (GHG) emissions. Companies currently voluntarily attempt to reduce carbon dioxide and GHG emissions (air pollution associated with climate change), yet many believe regulations will soon emerge in this area, thus, the field of carbon finance is poised for growth. Carbon finance encompasses various topics, such as cap-and-trade, carbon emissions trading, carbon tax, renewable energy certificates, and more.

Cap-and-Trade and Emissions Trading

A cap-and-trade system is an attempt to set a limit (a cap) on the amount of allowable carbon emissions from an industry, a geographic region, or a country. Companies are issued carbon permits for their share of allowable emissions. A company's goal would be to reduce emissions so as not to exceed its permits. Companies with fewer emissions than its permits can make money by selling their excess permits or carbon credits to another company; conversely, companies with more emissions than their permits allow must purchase additional permits. This gives rise to carbon trading, the buying and selling of company rights to emit carbon dioxide into the air. Carbon trading is a market-based mechanism to allocate carbon emissions allowances within the emissions trading system. It is speculated that the rise of a cap-and-trade system could also give rise to the creation of an economically viable carbon capture and storage industry. Carbon capture and storage involves removing carbon dioxide from fossil fuels before or after they are burned for energy. There are already a number of cap-and-trade systems in place that provide the mechanism for emissions trading markets (see chapter 2).

Carbon Tax

Levying a carbon pollution tax, or carbon tax, is one of the many options to lower carbon emissions. The tax is enacted upon the amount of carbon emissions and is reflective of the societal costs of carbon pollution. In a carbon tax, the government translates the price per ton of carbon into a tax on nonrenewable fuels, such as natural gas or oil. Rather than externalizing the costs of emissions from these energy sources, the carbon tax is an attempt to internalize costs and make consumers pay for the ultimate environmental damage resulting from the choice to use nonrenewable energy sources.

Sustainable Financing

Banks, credit unions, independent credit agencies, venture capitalists, and insurance companies are financial intermediaries that raise capital from investors and provide financing to operations with public and personal borrowing. Along with the wave of positive economic, social, and environment impact projects, government and financial institutions' attention has been drawn to the integration of green policies and practices for the financial services industry's operations, product offerings, distribution, and customer access to services. The insurance industry provides an excellent example of a proactive approach to ecologically friendly sustainability by offering green insurance to manage and reduce climate change risks.

Industry Principles and Standards

As a steward of the global economy, credit managers of financial institutions can base lending decisions on social, economical, and environmental guidelines that support sustainable businesses and their operations. There are two primary industry standards: the Equator Principles and the Wolfsberg Principles.

The Equator Principles. The Equator Principles promote social and environmental policies to increase the positive impacts on ecosystems and communities, offering a consistent approach to environmental sustainability and social management. Equator Principles relate to the management of social and environmental issues in project financing. An Equator Principles Financial Institution (EPFI) is a financial institution that has adopted and integrated all 10 Equator Principles. For any project financing deals above $10 million, EPFIs only provide financing to projects that are socially responsible and environmentally sound. The Equator Principles are used for establishing procedures and standards related to an EPFI's project financing activities. Currently, 65 international banks have become signatories to the Equator Principles.

The Wolfsberg Principles. With the concerted effort of 11 of the world's largest private banks and the anticorruption organization Transparency International, the Wolfsberg Anti-Money Laundering Principles for Private Banking (Wolfsberg Principles for short) were established in 2000. The Wolfsberg Principles provide guidelines specifically dealing with antimoney laundering, antiterrorism funding, and the identification and examination of unusual or suspicious activities. The principles also cover diverse policies that pertain to knowing your customers, especially for relationships between high net worth individuals and the financial institutions. So far, they are the best set of nonbinding guidelines concerning appropriate dealing between private bankers and global clients. Wolfsberg Principles deal primarily with appropriate monetary dealings between bankers and their customers.

A sustainability development program in banking would involve the adoption and incorporation of the Wolfsberg Principles and the Equator Principles into the banking business practices. The adoption of both of those principles by financial institutions gives rise to the opportunity for the provision of funding to ecologically friendly, socially disadvantaged, and economically underserved communities and sectors.

Sustainable Development Labeling Project. Significant progress has also been made to improve the quality of investment information provided by financial institutions. For example, French bank Caisse d'Epargne has recently launched a sustainable development labeling system, Bénéfices Futur, to rate savings, loan, and insurance products based on the impacts of financial risk, social responsibility, and ecological changes.[19] The labeling system ranks bank products based on green marketing of products, accessibility of products, and the bank's investments in and donations to socially responsible sectors and projects that support public interest causes. The labeling system also rates financial products that help to identify gaps between actual and perceived coverage and specify deductibles and effective time periods. Caisse d'Epargne's sharing of the labeling system with other banks facilitates the spread of sustainability efforts in the banking industry.

Categories of Sustainable Financing

Green financing. Sustainable financing can be classified as either green financing or social financing. Greenfinancing enables investors to finance green projects less expensively, by offering attractive financing, a lower interest rate or tax incentives, and rebates for environmentally friendly investments and investment in green funds or bonds. An energy-efficient mortgage (EEM) is an example of a green finance opportunity. In the EEM case, lenders can make an adjustment to the loan-to-value and stretch debt-to-income qualifying ratios for borrowers with energy-efficient houses because of the projected monthly energy savings. For widespread adoption of green projects, financial institutions, residents, builders, and local government need to be equipped with affordable sustainability knowledge and practical information on how to finance those projects.

Social finance. Apart from being green, sustainable finance also involves social finance activities that enhance local communities and social development. Social finance enables the channeling of investment capital to deliver positive social, economic, and environmental returns for the long run and for a global community. These channels include, but are not limited to, community investing, social enterprise lending, sustainable business, philanthropic grant making, and program-related investments. The Center for the Development of Social Finance is a nonprofit education and research organization that strives to expand awareness of social finance.

Microfinancing has gained great exposure recently as a special variety of social financing. Microfinancing is access to capital for women, minorities, and low-income borrowers who are not able to access loans from traditional resources. Microfinancing provides smaller loans with favorable terms and, for some programs, requires no or little collateral. Microfinancing seeks to aid in the revitalization of urban and rural communities.

Some states have sustainable microloan fund programs for underserved sectors, low-income communities, small businesses, and farmers. For example, the Strolling of the Heifer's microloan fund offers loans anywhere from $1,000 to $10,000 for terms up to 3 to 5 years. Despite the relatively low budget, such programs are a good investment in the future health of the entire serviced region.[20]

Microfinancing also involves making small loans (or microloans) to low-income businesses to stimulate economic growth in less developed countries. Grameen Bank, Kiva, and Prosper are examples of successful microfinance enterprises. Grameen Bank offers no-collateral microloans to 7.5 million women in Bangladesh. Dr. Muhammad Yunus, founder of Grameen Bank, won the Nobel Peace Prize in 2006 for this nonprofit microfinancing concept.

Both Kiva and Prosper provide Internet microcredit to support sustainable causes. Kiva enables quick access to funds for small entrepreneurs especially in Indonesia and India. The average loan from Kiva is around $110 to be repaid in 6 to 12 months with no interest charged. Fifty percent of those borrowers in India were able to graduate out of poverty with the help of Kiva.[21] Prosper links suppliers and demanders of funds in the developed and developing world.

Community Development Financial Institutions

As an integral member of communities, financial institutions provide support for sustainable community social and economic development and ecological conservation. Specializing in promoting economic and community development, Community Development Financial Institutions provide financing to small businesses and housing and community facilities projects that revitalize economically distressed communities. There are four types of community development financial institutions: community development banks, community development credit unions, community development loan funds, and community development venture capital companies.

Community Development Banks. Community development banks are for-profit banks committed to socially, economically, and environmentally sustainable community development. ShoreBank is the largest and most well-known community development bank in the United States and is the only one that takes into consideration all three dimensions of sustainability (social, economic, and environmental). ShoreBank opened in 1973 in Chicago and currently boasts $2.4 billion in assets and $4.2 million in net income with offices and businesses around the country and internationally; it is the nation's first community development and environmental banking corporation. ShoreBank defines its triple bottom line mission as profitability, community development impact, and conservation. Community development banks exist around the world, the most notable of which is Grameen Bank, as discussed under the topic of social finance.

Community Development Credit Unions. Community development credit unions (CDCU) are nonprofit, cooperatively owned, government-regulated, tax-exempt and insured financial institutions specializing in social financing. They serve low- and moderate-income people and communities by providing below-market-rate small loans to imperfect or no credit history borrowers and by offering financial education for its members. Major funding for CDCU institutions comes from banks, foundations, and other investors for deposits to support their work. Through partnerships with the private sector and participation in outreach and government programs, CDCU institutions are able to leverage community revitalization efforts. Federally chartered CDCU institutions are state regulated.

Community Development Loan Funds. Community development loan funds provide loan funds for businesses, nonprofits, and underserved areas for the purpose of economic development. Loan funds provide financing to traditionally unqualified borrowers who would use the funds for advancing sustainable actions. These loan funds require collateral, but they have flexible payment schedules. The government's sustainable development loan fund offers low interest loans up to $500,000 to businesses for green projects like utilizing sustainable resources, producing recyclable finished products, and installing pollution prevention procedures.

Community Development Venture Capital. Community development venture capital (CDVC) funds provide equity capital to entrepreneurial companies that will ultimately benefit low-income people and distressed communities. The amount of the investment funding from CDVC funds is generally less than that of their traditional counterparts. The average CDVC fund investment for small businesses was about $331,000 per company in 2000.[22] Kentucky Highlands Investment Corporation (KHIC) runs a very successful rural economic development program. KHIC's ventures contribute at least 68% of the net growth of manufacturing jobs in Kentucky Highland's nine target counties from 1970 to 1990. The positive entrepreneurial capitalism spurs from the enhanced availability of community venture financing.[23]

Sustainable Insurance

The insurance industry is particularly interested in sustainability, given the impact that climate change has had on this industry's profitability. In fact, climate change is the number one risk to the insurance industry.[24] According to an Ernst & Young study,[25] climate change could result in increased mortality and health problems, increased environmentally related litigation, increased conflicts over control of resources, and negative impacts on capital markets.

According to a 2005 study by the Association of British Insurers, if carbon dioxide emission levels are doubled, the capital requirement for insurers could increase by $76 billion, which is an 80%–90% increase due to the increased risk of tropical cyclones in the United States and Japan.[26] Allianz, Europe's largest insurer, estimated that losses due to climate change could be as high as $400 billion. In addition to property loss, insured companies may face carbon-regulatory risks governing its investment and insurance policies on green projects. Given these challenges, the industry is addressing the concept of sustainability and is taking notice of social, environmental, and economic impacts.

Many insurers have increased their focus on financial risk management. Yet proactive insurers are making progress in developing both investment strategies to "participate in the 'green' revolution in the financial markets" and in creating new climate-friendly products to address climate change risk.[27] Many of these financial products deal with green building, hurricane-resistant design, promotion of alternate fuels, and sustainable driving practices to reduce carbon emissions. Proactive insurers encourage the insured to participate in the insurance sustainability effort.

Insurance companies play an important role in social, economic, and ecologically friendly sustainability. Swiss Re has sold weather-risk products to 320,000 small farmers in India. For renewable energy-related insurance products, Willis Holdings covers potential power underproduction of wind farms. As a pioneer in offering green-building policies, Lexington Insurance Company's new policies will pay the insured to rebuild a home using environmentally friendly and energy-efficient materials after it is destroyed by natural disasters.[28]

In Japan, Sompo Japan Insurance and Tokio Marine Nichido Fire Insurance Co., Ltd. have given premium discounts to 10 million policyholders who drive low-emitting cars. Travelers and Farmers cut 10% off the policy premium for hybrid cars. Progressive and GMAC insurance companies offer pay-as-you-drive (PAYD) policies in parts of the United States. In the U.S., automobiles account for 25% of all GHG emissions and it is anticipated that implementing PAYD policies and hybrid vehicle incentives could reduce emissions by 10%.[29]

Increasingly, insurance companies have utilized exclusion clauses—tightened conditions to foster the right decisions by customers. Some insurance companies limit liabilities for emitters of greenhouse gases and for companies that do not have a climate mitigation plan in place. "Development and establishment of business-continuity management (BCM) procedures [is used as] a prerequisite for adding on business interruption coverage to a company's property insurance."[30] As one of the world's largest re-insurers, Swiss Re, Munich Re requires disclosure of a company's climate strategy in their directors and officers insurance application.[31]

As this chapter has demonstrated, the finance function, as well as the finance industry, is greatly impacted by sustainability considerations. Every aspect of finance, from investments to banking and from trading to insurance and risk, requires new thinking when we consider the social, economic, and environmental impact of business.

CHAPTER 5

Research and Development

Growing public pressures, stricter enforcement of environmental laws, costly cleanup costs, limited resources, and less disposal options are creating the need for research and development (R&D) departments to rethink plans, policies, and procedures. The unique nature of R&D activities makes planning sustainable efforts extremely difficult. This chapter discusses several concepts (cradle to cradle, biomimicry, life cycle assessment, and crowdsourcing) that facilitate meaningful R&D for sustainability.

Cradle to Cradle

Products and processes have historically been designed for cradle to grave. That is, design has only considered the product from the point of manufacture to disposal. With growing awareness of environmental impacts and companies' tendency to externalize costs, there has been a shift in thinking about design in terms of cradle to cradle, or from the point of acquisition of raw materials to the point of recycle and reuse.[1] Cradle to cradle design requires a shift in thinking about traditional manufacturing, recycling, and environmentalism. Cradle to cradle design encourages us not to choose the least environmentally damaging approach but rather to create and design a better approach. Cradle to cradle design encourages the integration of nature into the design process with a goal of zero waste. Products and processes integrating this design philosophy can receive Cradle to Cradle certification.[2]

Biomimicry

Biomimicry is an innovative method that searches for sustainable solutions by imitating features naturally found in the environment into the design of products. Using biomimicry, sustainable businesses can look at nature in new ways to understand how it can be used to help solve problems. Nature can be seen in three different perspectives: nature as model, nature as measure, and nature as mentor.[3] Nature as model implies the emulation of forms, processes, or systems in product design. Nature as measure implies the evaluation of what is being designed against criteria of nature to see if current methods are as efficient as those from nature. Nature as mentor means creating a bond or relationship with nature, treating nature as a partner and teacher rather than just a place for resource removal.[4]

Many industries have benefited from biomimicry. In the transportation industry, the fastest train in the world, the Shinkansen Bullet Train of the Japan Railways Group, incorporated biomimicry design methods into its revised design. With the initial design of the train, a loud noise was produced when the bullet train emerged from a tunnel. Designers redesigned the nose of the train after the beak of a kingfisher, which dives into water to catch fish. Not only did the modification create a quieter train, but it also resulted in less electricity usage and faster travel time.[5] This is an excellent example of utilizing nature to improve engineering.

Another example is GreenShield, a fabric finish made by G3i, which provides the same water and stain repellency as conventional fabric finishes with 8 times fewer harmful chemicals.[6] The innovation was developed from the water repellency of the leaves of a lotus plant. The plant's surface texture traps air so that water droplets float and slide off cleanly while removing the dirt.

After studying the flippers, fins, and tails of whales, dolphins, and sharks, the company WhalePower applied biomimicry to design a far more efficient wind turbine blade with less drag, increased lift, and delayed stall. The company expects to apply its design to fan blades of all types to gain up to 20% increased efficiencies and quieter operations.[7]

The air conditioning system of Eastgate Building, an office building in Zimbabwe, was modeled from self-cooling mounds made by termites. The building uses 90% less energy than conventional buildings of the same size, and the owners have been able to spend $3.5 million less on air-conditioning costs.[8]

These are but a few examples of the many improvements in design that have been brought about through biomimicry, or nature-inspired design. Sustainable businesses can find workshops, research reports, biological consulting, field excursions, and other resource information from the Biomimicry Guild, an environmental consultation firm, and from the Biomimicry Institution, a nonprofit advocacy group. The Institute has developed an online interactive resource, AskNature.org,[9] which allows users to pose a problem, and feedback is provided in the form of multiple ideas or examples from nature that might be useful in solving the problem.

Life Cycle Analysis

As environmental awareness becomes more prevalent, businesses are assessing how their activities affect the environment. The environmental performance of products and processes has become a key issue, which is why some companies are investigating ways to minimize effects on the environment. Life cycle analysis (LCA, sometimes referred to as life cycle assessment) measures the environmental impact of specific products or processes from cradle to grave. Cradle to grave begins with the gathering of raw materials from the earth to create the product and ends at the point of materials disposal, recycle, or reuse (although LCA uses the term cradle to grave, recycle and reuse scenarios can be built into the analysis for a more accurate cradle to cradle analysis). LCA provides a snapshot in time of a specific product from a specific manufacturer, and it may be difficult to generalize findings. However, LCA is a useful tool for making product and process decisions that consider environmental criteria. The benefit of LCA is that businesses can identify the most effective improvements to reduce cumulative environmental impacts resulting from all stages in the product life cycle, often including upstream and downstream impacts not considered in more traditional analyses (e.g., raw material extraction, material transportation, ultimate product disposal, etc.). LCA is widely used for different purposes by different groups: environmental groups use it to inform consumers on what to buy, legislators use it for creating rules and regulations, and manufacturers use it as they seek to improve design and production standards. Less commonly used methods for environmental comparisons include value–impact assessments, environmental option assessments, and impact analysis matrices.

The LCA process is a systematic phased set of stages and is comprised of four components: goal definition and scoping, inventory analysis, impact assessment, and interpretation. The first stage is goal definition and scoping, which identifies the purpose of the analysis and the context in which the assessment will be conducted. In defining the scope of the LCA, it is important to define the system boundaries. The system boundaries can affect the outcomes of an LCA. Therefore, when comparing multiple products, such as plastic versus corn-based disposable cutlery, it is essential to ensure that the same system boundaries are used to examine both. A functional unit needs to be selected, such as a box of cereal, or a bar of soap, or a ton of grain. The definition of the boundaries should include where the material is extracted (the cradle) and what is the final disposal point for the product (the grave).

The next stage is the inventory analysis where data is collected related to energy, water, and materials usage. LCA includes an analysis of what has been used from the environment, such as raw materials, and what has been released into the environment, such as GHG emissions, solid waste disposal, and wastewater discharges. When moving to the inventory analysis stage, sustainable companies find it much easier to envision the system boundaries for data collection by developing a model of the life cycle or a flow diagram. A flow diagram is a map depicting inputs and outputs within the system boundaries. The diagram allows the investigator to break down the system into a set of subsystems that represent particular phases of the life cycle and shows linkages across these phases.[10] For example, the flow chart may include raw material extraction, raw material processing, transportation, manufacture, production fabrication, filling and packaging, assembly, distribution, use, reuse, maintenance, recycle, and waste disposal. The focus of the inventory analysis is data collection of the raw material and energy consumption and emissions to air, water, and land. Data can be collected from various sources.

Suppliers of materials and energy as well as consultants specializing in sustainability can provide valuable information. Other sources that can provide information are government and industrial databases, government reports, existing LCA reports, and laboratory test data. LCA, though very valuable to sustainable businesses, is complex and labor intensive. Software is available to eliminate the need to conduct complex

calculations. A sample of LCA software tools can be found at the following Web site: http://www.life-cycle.org/LCA_soft.htm.[11]

The two final stages, life cycle impact analysis and interpretation, evaluate the effects of resources and emissions identified in the previous stage. The
third stage uses the findings of the inventory analysis to conduct an impact
analysis that considers the consequential effects on population and ecology.
Impact analysis provides quantifiable impact information on such issues as
environmental and human health, resource depletion, and social welfare. The
steps that have been identified with the impact analysis stage are identifying relevant environment impact categories, for example, global warming or
acidification; classification or classifying carbon dioxide in relation to global
warming; characterization or modeling the potential impact of carbon dioxide on global warming; describing impacts in ways for comparison; sorting
and ranking indicators; weighting the most important impacts; and evaluating the results.[12] The final stage is to interpret the findings from the previous
stages to make informed decisions for products and processes.[13]

The greatest benefit of an LCA is that is allows scientific comparison
of products or processes in order to determine the most environmentally
friendly option from cradle to grave. This scientific evidence may or may
not support our beliefs about the best choice among options (see Table 5.1).
However, the limitations of LCA studies should be understood when
interpreting results. LCA studies are a static profile capturing the qualities
of a specific product at that moment in time. The studies are constrained
by the product (or process) selected, the manufacturer selected, its manufacturing practices, its supply chain practices, and the other boundaries of
scope defined at the onset of the study. In addition, there are numerous
approaches to the use of LCA, which further restrict comparison of studies. For example, depending on the purpose of the LCA, researchers may
opt to use economic input–output LCA, screening LCA, process LCA,
hybrid LCA, full-product LCA, financial LCA, life cycle energy analysis,
or other specific approaches. As such, there exists much controversy over
LCA study results as an indication of eco-friendliness.[14] Furthermore, there
is criticism that LCA studies only focus on environmental aspects and
neglect other aspects of sustainability. While not a perfect method, LCA
is the best model that exists for considering the environmental impact of
products, processes, and services.

Table 5.1. Test Your Knowledge
Based on the results of life cycle analysis (LCA) studies,* which is the more environmentally friendly choice?

1.	**Paper or Styrofoam cup?** LCA research shows production of Styrofoam is less energy and water intensive than paper cups and that production of paper cups creates more greenhouse gas (GHG) emissions.[a] The conclusion: Styrofoam is better from an environmental standpoint, but neither is ideal.[b]
2.	**Stainless steel coffee mug or ceramic mug or Styrofoam cup?** LCA research shows a reusable ceramic mug is more environmentally friendly than Styrofoam *as long as it is used at least 46 times* (that's 46 cups of coffee!).[c] The LCA also shows that a stainless steel mug must be used at least 396 times to be more environmentally friendly than Styrofoam.[d]
3.	**Biodegradable to-go food containers or Styrofoam?** LCA research shows biodegradable bioplastic containers made from corn or other agricultural products create more GHG emissions than Styrofoam.[e]
4.	**Bioplastic disposable cutlery or plastic?** LCA research shows that bioplastic products made from corn or other agricultural products (such as PLA or PHA) require more energy and produce more GHG emissions in manufacturing than do petroleum-based plastic cutlery.[f]
5.	**Biodegradable or plastic or paper bags?** LCA research shows that plastic bags produce the least environmental impact in manufacturing, transportation, and recycling.[g]

* Since the time of the studies mentioned here, products and processes may have improved, thus impacting the results if another LCA study were to be conducted today. Updated LCA studies are needed.

[a] Haag, Maloney, and Ward (2006).

[b] Haag et al. (2006).

[c] Paster (2006).

[d] Paster (2006).

[e] Athena Sustainable Materials Institute (2006).

[f] Gerngross and Slater (2000).

[g] Lilienfeld (2007).

As an example, an LCA of PLA (a corn-based bioplastic manufactured by Dow Chemicals's NatureWorks, LLC) versus plastic found that the manufacture of plastic was less energy intensive, thus emitting fewer greenhouse gases during the manufacturing process, and that the plastic manufacturing process required less water. Therefore, the conclusion was that plastic was a better choice than PLA from an environmental impact standpoint. However, when the manufacturer of PLA, Nature-Works LLC, began purchasing wind power carbon offsets in 2006, the company's LCA studies suggested that NatureWorks's PLA was now the better choice from an environmental impact standpoint.[15] Others have disagreed with these results based on the argument that the purchase of wind power carbon offsets, or the investment in another company's wind power project, does not bring the wind power to the NatureWorks manufacturing facility and, as such, does not reduce the intensity of the electricity consumption during the PLA manufacturing process.[16] As this example demonstrates, LCA studies compare a specific product and determines its impact at that point in time, given the manufacturer, its various processes, and the boundaries defined for the study. This limits generalization of the findings to similar products by other manufacturers.

Crowdsourcing

Organizations have long used techniques such as brainstorming, the Delphi technique, and quality circles for employees and managers to generate creative solutions to problems. Crowdsourcing[17] is a similar idea on a larger scale using the Web to reach a larger set of problem solvers. Problems are made available via the Internet in the form of an open call for solutions. Participants (the crowd) may be customers, suppliers, employees, member communities, or simply the general public. The participants suggest solutions to the problem, discuss their merits or disadvantages, and select favorite choices. Participants can be motivated to do so through awards, recognition, or financial compensation. Participants are potential end users of the product and are generally willing to provide ideas and solutions from that aspect.

Sustainable businesses can benefit from crowdsourcing, which also has been referred to as community-based design, as a substitute for in-house R&D to reduce overhead and staffing expenses. Businesses can create their own online crowdsourcing site or they can utilize one of the many links that are currently available. Online discussion and voting from the community at large provides results similar to company-driven marketing research. Companies can obtain feedback, ideas, and solutions from a wider range of talent, which can conceivably develop better products with faster time to market and at lower costs.

As an example, InnoCentive provides outsource research functions to a variety of disciplines such as life sciences, computer science, business and entrepreneurship, engineering, and chemistry. Sustainable organizations can register with InnoCentive as solution seekers, while individuals can register as solvers. Organizations post a dilemma or problem for which they are seeking a solution, and the open community of solvers is available to offer suggestions and solutions.

For example, SunNight Solar developed solar-powered flashlights for use in developing countries and areas without electricity. The initial design provided task lighting, but the goal was to create another design to replace kerosene lanterns (a safety and environmental hazard) and to illuminate entire rooms. After several failed design attempts, SunNight Solar CEO Mark Bent turned to InnoCentive and put forth the design challenge to InnoCentive's social network of over 140,000 solvers. The challenge was solved and the new SL-2 light, or Super BOGO, was sent into production.

Other crowdsourcing venues that outsource for a broad range of industries or disciplines include Innovation Exchange, NineSigma, Fellowforce, and Yet2.com.[18] CrowdSPRING[19] focuses on contributions for logo design, business card design, graphic design, Web site design, and photography. Amazon created a platform called the Amazon Mechanical Turk[20] on which tasks called "HITs" (Human Intelligence Tasks) can be made public for people to work on and receive compensation.

As with other functions of the business, sustainability brings new ways of thinking to the task of R&D. From the way products are designed to the way research is conducted and problems are solved, sustainability challenges our old mindsets.

CHAPTER 6

Marketing

No product, regardless of how well it is designed, will reach consumers unless it is marketed effectively. The marketing function is an important component of any business. It is involved in the development, communication, and provision of value to consumers of the firm's products or services. This chapter demonstrates how sustainability efforts are integrated across the marketing mix: product, price, place (distribution), and promotion.

Product

The first element of the marketing mix is the product. The sustainable business addresses issues related to the product's design, packaging, and branding.

Sustainable businesses focus on green product design and development, as discussed in chapter 5. Green product design and development engages in design for the environment, sustainable product architectures, design for flexibility and reuse, green product testing, design for recycling, and life cycle analysis (LCA) for sustainability.

In designing for the environment, the sustainable business will become familiar with the International Organization for Standardization (ISO) 14000 standards, which focus on environmental management issues. The standards are quality guidelines for companies to continuously identify, control, and improve environmental performance. The sustainable business will take steps to create conditions to assure product testing does not cause unnecessary and harmful social or environmental impacts. Design for recycling, flexibility, and reuse not only reduces environmental impact but can also create cost efficiencies for the organization. It is important that the company conduct LCA on products and processes (discussed in chapter 5). LCA is a method to better understand the impact of a product, service, or process throughout the entire duration of its life from acquisition of raw materials to use or reuse and to its eventual disposal.

Sustainability can also be applied to service design. Businesses providing services such as hospitals, hotels, and restaurants will focus on issues such as minimizing nonrenewable energy consumption, protecting water sources, enhancing the indoor air quality for the consumer, and using environmentally preferable products in providing those services.

A sustainable business also increases efforts to reduce waste and environmental impact through product packaging. Reducing the size of the package or redesigning the shape may result in increased efficiencies in storage and transportation. Eliminating plastic wrap or liners from products will reduce the amount of waste transferred to the landfill. Furthermore, biodegradable, recyclable, and reusable materials for packaging will significantly reduce the long-term environmental impact of packaging. Lastly, the packaging material itself may be altered.

Wal-Mart Stores, Inc. (and Sam's West, Inc.) was the first to implement a packaging scorecard to evaluate the impact of packaging from suppliers. The scorecard criteria cover such items as greenhouse gas/carbon dioxide (GHG/CO_2) emissions per ton of production, product–package ratio, cube utilization, recycled content, renewable energy, and transportation. Businesses using a packaging scorecard have an objective measure of commitment to sustainability efforts and can inform suppliers of the commitment to sustainable packaging.

Another packaging inroad is the concept of eco-labeling. An eco-label is a label or symbol, such as ENERGY STAR, EcoLogo, or Green Seal, that educates and informs the buyer of certain environmental claims. Sustainable businesses are urged to use industry-wide labels, standardized by ISO 14024 regulations, which are generally recognized by the public versus proprietary labels that do not carry the same credibility factor. Other types of eco-labels may provide information on the product through its life cycle, such as the origin and history of the product or the amount of greenhouse gas emissions created in production. This approach is currently being used in Patagonia's Footprint Chronicles and Wal-Mart's Love, Earth jewelry line. Consumers are able to track the life of the product from raw materials to retail sale.

Lastly, any business should avoid the use of vague terms on packaging, such as green, nonpolluting, natural, eco-friendly, and others. If using such terms, a business should be ready to provide evidence to support its claims. This includes full awareness and understanding of processes and product supply chains. For example, a company that claims its organic product was produced without chemicals or pesticides may find that contaminants have crept in from processing or transport and have made the claim ultimately false. Such vagueness has the potential to be misinterpreted and misunderstood in numerous ways by consumers.

A company will develop a brand in order to give its company and its products an identity. Branding builds an emotional bond or connection with the consumer, and with that bond an organization can obtain loyalty from the consumer. Sufficient consideration should be given to determine a brand name or symbol that identifies the brand with the company's sustainability philosophy and that captures the essence of the sustainable properties of the product. A sustainable business will have the triple bottom line (people, planet, profit) at the base of its branding. Sustainability and branding should provide a seamlessly integrated front. Separated from each other, branding faces the risk of becoming irrelevant or overlooked. Green companies will also want to differentiate themselves from other green companies on the basis of their sustainability. As an increasing number of organizations go green, it will become increasingly important to set themselves and their marketing efforts apart from the competition.

Price

Pricing is a major element in sustainability marketing. Issues such as price elasticity, premium pricing, and perceived value pricing will be discussed in relation to pricing for sustainability.

In the past, environmental and social costs were considered external to the production costs and had not, by general rule, been included in consideration of setting prices. However, as stakeholders and legislation increase demands on the companies to provide more sustainable solutions, companies have been driven to consider these costs within pricing policies. Sustainable companies reexamine costing methods (as discussed in chapter 4 and chapter 8) and begin to consider the real and actual social, economic, and environmental costs associated with products and services.

The demand for environmentally friendly products is inelastic, for the most part, meaning that a change in the price has little or no effect on the quantity that consumers are willing to buy. Consumers have generally been willing to pay a slight green premium, or higher price, for environmentally friendly products. Through premium pricing, sustainable businesses can continue to invest in innovations and development of sustainable processes. However, premium pricing does not have to be the case. In chapter 2, there are several considerations to help the sustainable business reduce costs through increased efficiency and reduced waste. When the sustainable business is successful in reducing costs from these efficiencies, it will have more flexibility in pricing policies.

Consumers have also become very knowledgeable and aware of sustainability alternatives and issues in recent times. When considering pricing strategies, companies need to be committed to ensuring that its sustainable products perform beyond or at least as good as those products that do not make sustainability claims. Companies may want to use perceived value pricing, which is a market-based approach to pricing as opposed to pricing based on the cost to make the product. The price is set by estimating the perceptions of the consumer regarding the benefit they think they will receive from the product or service.

Place (Distribution)

After producing the product, business must distribute the goods and services to the consumer. A sustainable business will want to create an efficient distribution system. In particular, logistics plays a vital part in the distribution system. Logistics is the freight transport of goods and services from manufacturer to distributor and onward to point of consumption.

The sustainable business may be interested in collaborative planning, forecasting, and replenishment, which focuses on information sharing among trading partners in order to develop a joint market plan. Not only can businesses share information, but they can also share transportation, warehousing, and infrastructure. The use of just-in-time electronic data interchange and electronic point-of-sale concepts by sustainable businesses allows ordering and stocking to be more cost effective and timely, which creates replenishment efficiencies in the system. Companies hold less stock, it is shipped only when needed, and this reduces unnecessary shipping.

Reverse logistics is another concept that has arisen from the increase in efforts to reduce waste. Reverse logistics is the movement of a product backward through the supply channel to be reused, recycled, or reprocessed. Sustainable companies should create a continuous process that plans for products to be flagged for recycling or reuse at whatever point is most efficient. Agents in the chain should be identified that are in a position to collect the used products, classify and sort them, and then transport them back to the manufacturer. Kodak, the manufacturer of cameras, is very successful using reverse logistics and remanufacturing for their single-use cameras through retail photo processing. Another company, Lexmark, a printer and toner cartridge manufacturer, creates a process in which the customer is responsible for reverse logistics through rebate programs and incentives for returning used cartridges.[1]

Freight is transported via various means such as roadways, waterways, railways, and air travel. Each has its advantages and disadvantages. The sustainable business will examine the viability of using efficient forms of travel, such as rail or waterways, to transport the product whenever possible. These forms can provide efficiencies in transportation costs by transporting more of the product at one time versus multiple transports by road with smaller loads. In addition, fewer loads result in fewer road accidents, which impact the triple bottom line from a social perspective.

Roadway travel is by far the slowest means and, from a sustainability standpoint, it is also the most inefficient. When using the roadway for transport, the sustainable business will conduct transportation modeling solutions to determine the most efficient distribution system in order to minimize distances and transportation costs. Transport systems many times will be only partially loaded or even empty if precision in planning is not accomplished. The sustainable business may be able to collaborate with other businesses to maximize transportation loading in both directions where feasible. In addition, distribution facilities should be centrally located to minimize travel distances.

In order to reduce emissions, the transportation fleet should be periodically checked for fuel efficiencies and emission performance. Fleet carriers should not be allowed to idle when not moving (traveling), which unnecessarily uses excessive fuel. In order for internal systems to operate, such as radios, air-conditioning, and refrigeration, trucks typically have had to keep engines idling. IdleAire manufactures a system that provides truck stops with a power grid for truck hookup. The grid provides power to the trucks while they are parked. Using this product, the state of New York expects to reduce emissions from commercial truck idling by 98%.[2]

The sustainable business should also plan routes for maximum efficiency, such as UPS's right-turn-only policy, and include stop points at diesel stations that have truck stop electrification to provide trucks with grid-based electricity. Companies that ship both refrigerated and non-refrigerated products may consider dual temperature vehicles that move both product types in the same shipment and decrease the need for separate carriage.

Another example of transportation innovations in product distribution can be found at Unilever HLL's subsidiary in India. The company's laboratories developed a method that allows ice cream to be transported cheaply throughout the country in nonrefrigerated trucks. This innovation significantly reduced electricity consumption, eliminated the need for refrigerants, and was cheaper than previous transportation methods.[3]

Promotion

Companies engage in promotion of products and services through advertising, public relations, word of mouth, and point of sale. The following paragraphs will discuss selected topics related to sustainable marketing promotion, such as advertising issues, cause-related marketing, sustainable promotional products, and greenwashing concerns.

Advertising is the most familiar element of promotion to reach potential customers. Businesses use sales promotions, personal selling, direct marketing, and public relations to communicate their message to potential customers. Market segment groups identified as particularly attractive for the sustainable business include Lifestyles of Health and Sustainability (LOHAS) and Cultural Creatives. The LOHAS segment of the population is described as individuals committed to health, the environment, social justice, personal development, and sustainable living. The Cultural Creatives segment of the population is described as individuals committed to spirituality, social justice, and environmentalism. Together, they represent a sizable and growing percentage of our population.

Whether a business specifically targets LOHAS or Cultural Creatives segments of the population or targets the general population, consumers are attracted to ethical marketing practices. A sustainable business often engages in cause-related marketing, or connecting its branding image with certain causes to which consumers will strongly relate. For the sustainable business, the cause is sustainability, and therefore it is critical to communicate the social and environmental benefits of products. It is also important that consumers are able to see a clear connection between the company (or its brand image) and the charitable cause it supports. When consumers consider the product, the corporation's ethics and values are reflected in its choices of charitable causes and they are transparent to the consumer.

Two specific types of cause-related marketing are green marketing and social marketing. Green marketing refers to the marketing of products or services that are environmentally friendly. The U.S. Trade Commission and the Canadian Standards Association both provide guidelines for making environmental claims of products. Social marketing refers to marketing of products or services for social good. Sustainable businesses often partner with nonprofit organizations to promote social change or to donate a percentage of profit to these organizations. Well-known examples include the partnerships between Susan G. Komen for the Cure and (PRODUCT) RED and the various businesses that support these causes. Due to the emotional connections in linking a cause with a brand, consumer response may actually be stronger through these forms of cause-related marketing than by advertising alone.

Additional marketing promotion considerations are the marketing materials and promotional items. Marketing materials (including business cards) and promotional items will reflect the sustainable business's commitment to environmental and social responsibility. Marketing materials and items used by the sustainable business do not produce waste, require fewer resources in production, are recycled and reusable, are biodegradable, use soy-based inks, use nontoxic components, and avoid

PVC plastic and other harmful materials. Examples of eco-friendly pro-motional products are items made from PLA, a corn-based biodegradable plastic (such as pens or coffee mugs); organic products (such as T-shirts and bags); recycled products (such as mouse pads, umbrellas, and cloth-ing); and renewable energy powered products (such as solar-powered or water-powered flashlights, calculators, and radios).

There are numerous communication channels to reach sustainability-minded consumers and to promote your sustainability message. See Table 6.1 for a small sample of the many print and online outlets for both advertising and press releases.

Table 6.1. Promote Your Sustainability Message
There are many print and online media outlets to reach sustainability-minded consumers, such as

Business Ethics Magazine
ClimateChangeCorp
Corporate Knights
CSRwire
Environmental Leader
Environmental News Network
Ethical Corporation
GOOD Magazine
GreenMoney Journal
Greener World Media and its associated sites (such as GreenBiz)
Grist Magazine
LOHAS Journal
Matter Network
Mother Jones Earth
NEED Magazine
Plenty Magazine
Sustainable Business Design Blog
Sustainable Industries
TreeHugger
Triple Pundit
World Business Council for Sustainable Development

The sustainable business's marketing emphasis will be on openness, honesty, and transparency in any product or company claims. An effort to promote a single token product or act of a company as sustainable, green, or environmentally friendly will be met with skepticism by critics and will earn the company a reputation of greenwashing. Greenwashing is the act of creating an environmental spin on products or activities without genuine business-wide commitment to sustainability. Sustainability is a company-wide goal that permeates through every task, role, department, division, and activity of the company. Unwitting businesses may engage in greenwashing for a variety of reasons, such as a lack of understanding of sustainability. Other reasons may include attempts to expand market share, attract and manage employees, attract investors, derail critics, circumvent regulatory issues, and improve image. However, greenwashing may damage an otherwise credible business's image or reputation.

The sustainable business can circumvent greenwashing by avoiding vague terms (such as green, nonpolluting, and eco-friendly), providing substantial evidence to support any sustainability claims, staying clear of irrelevant claims, and by providing specific details to curtail misunderstandings. Partnering with one's harshest critics and nongovernmental organizations, such as Environmental Defense Fund, American Red Cross, National Wildlife Foundation, and ClimateGroup, may provide the organization some guidance in making meaningful progress toward sustainability and in creating positive impressions.

Suspect greenwashing can draw attention and can subject companies to violations of various federal and state laws. In particular, the Federal Trade Commission (FTC) Act set forth Green Guides in 1992 and revised them in 1998 to provide basic principles on what is permissible in green marketing claims. Due to the nature of guidelines, which are not legally binding, there has been little enforcement for companies to closely follow the guidelines. However, the FTC's task is to monitor and prevent unfair deceptive practices and to bring action against a company if they believe it has committed deceptive practices. The criteria for deceptive practices are based on whether a claim can be substantiated, whether the claim is vague and misleading, and whether the claim provides an overstatement of environmental benefits.

Due to the rise in green marketing claims, the FTC is in the process of again updating the guidelines. A new chair of the FTC, William Kovacic, has been appointed and appears to be a strong advocate of addressing greenwashing. Companies are likely to observe stronger enforcement of the FTC Act with regard to greenwashing. The FTC has been holding public meetings on topics related to green marketing, such as green buildings, carbon offsets, and renewable energy certificates. The revised Green Guides are to be released in 2009.

In addition to FTC Green Guides for businesses, several third-party Web sites seek to help consumers identify cases of greenwashing. GreenPeace offers a Greenwash Detection Kit,[4] TerraChoice details the Six Sins of Greenwashing,[5] CorpWatch tracks offenders through its Greenwash Awards[6] and related publications,[7] and EnviroMedia Social Marketing and the University of Oregon maintain the Greenwashing Index.[8] The FTC and third parties are each placing growing emphasis on separating greenwashing from authentic green claims.

This chapter has shown that sustainability impacts marketing decisions made within the standard marketing mix of product, price, place, and distribution. Sustainable businesses will design, package, brand, price, distribute, and promote products and services with social, economic, and environmental impacts in mind.

CHAPTER 7

Information Technology and Management Information Systems

Technology holds increasing promise in helping organizations become more efficient and environmentally friendly. In addition, sustainability requires transparency of social, environmental, and economic impacts (in an effort to prevent or expose illegal or unethical practices while increasing trust), and this transparency requires access to information. These needs put information professionals in a central position to help further the company's sustainability goals, either through technology or through management of information.

Information Technology

According to a recent study,[1] the carbon dioxide (CO_2) emissions of the U.S. information technology (IT) industry already exceed the emissions of entire nations, such as Argentina, the Netherlands, and Malaysia. At the current pace, emissions are expected to quadruple and the IT industry is expected to exceed the airline industry in emissions by 2020. The research shows that the U.S. IT industry is increasing its energy usage at a rate of 10%–20% annually. The study estimates that at this rising rate of energy usage, the United States will need to build 30 new coal-fired or nuclear power plants by 2015 solely to support the nation's IT usage.

The Smart 2020 report[2] estimates that IT has the potential to reduce worldwide global emissions by 15% by 2020. According to this report, the greatest global opportunities for IT to help reduce emissions are in the areas of smart motor systems in China's manufacturing industry, smart logistics in Europe's transport and storage industries, smart building technologies in North America, and smart grid technologies in India.

In order to address growing concerns over the environmental impact of the IT industry and to take advantage of opportunities, the proactive and sustainability-focused business will develop green IT strategies. Green IT strategies are not only proactive and environmentally friendly but can also ultimately reduce the company's energy consumption and costs.

There are a number of suggestions for green IT strategies. For example, the same McKinsey & Company[3] study suggests that most companies could double energy efficiency of data centers by 2012. The researchers propose automobile CAFE-type industry standards (corporate average fuel economy [CAFE] standards require an automaker to meet minimum average fuel efficiency across its entire fleet of manufactured vehicles). These CAFE-type industry standards would be used for measuring efficiency in conjunction with the following suggestions: creating an energy-efficiency dashboard, sealing cable cutoffs, turning off and removing excess hardware, increasing temperatures, virtualization, and upgrading equipment.

Greening the data center is often the starting point of green IT strategies. The first step in your green IT strategy is to know current energy usage, where energy is used and by what specific equipment, what usage is efficient, and what usage is wasteful. There are a number of IT-enabled energy-reduction systems (such as EnviroCube or EnerSure monitoring devices or Verdiem software tools), smart metering, and other technologies that can ultimately reduce cooling costs and electricity consumption. As if that is not incentive enough, the U.S. Environmental Protection Agency (EPA) is currently developing an ENERGY STAR rating for data center infrastructure, and the European Commission has developed a Code of Conduct for Green Data Centers. We will now look at some specific green IT strategies designed to increase efficiency and decrease energy consumption.

Storage

Storage resource management (SRM) helps identify underutilized capacity, removes or reassigns unused storage, identifies old or noncritical data that could be moved to less expensive storage, removes inappropriate data, and helps predict future capacity requirements. SRM can increase storage utilization and decrease power needs. Companies that have used SRM have experienced utilization improvements of 30%–40%.[4]

Storage virtualization allows the work of several storage networks and devices to be integrated to appear as one virtual storage site. Storage virtualization can improve storage utilization by allowing storage to be assigned where it is needed.

Another tool is continuous data protection, which offers continuous or real-time byte-level backup of changes to documents. This often requires less storage space than traditional file-level backups.

Yet another option for reducing storage costs is storage tiering. Tiered storage assigns categories of data to specific types of storage media. The categories are company-defined based on levels of security and protection, usage, performance, or other considerations. This process can be automatically managed through software programs. The benefit of tiered storage is that it allows companies to increase utilization rates and decrease power consumption and cooling costs.

Servers

One green IT approach being used is server consolidation, which reduces the number of servers used by running multiple applications on each server. Another approach to reducing energy usage and increasing energy efficiency is server virtualization. Similar to storage virtualization discussed earlier, server virtualization allows virtual machines to run on one piece of hardware, at both the server and PC level.

Cloud computing is an option that allows access to computer technology via the Internet without your company purchasing or managing the technology. Cloud computing can be used with data centers, networks, configuration, software, hardware, infrastructure, platforms, services, and storage. Cloud computing can ultimately reduce costs while increasing utilization and efficiency. The FTC and computing professionals are beginning to address security issues in this new arena of cloud computing.[5]

Desktops

Green PCs are designed to minimize the use of electricity and to meet the Environmental Protection Agency's ENERGY STAR standards (new ENERGY STAR standards for computers were updated in 2007). One example is thin clients, diskless machines that consume a fraction of the power of standard desktop machines. The average desktop computer uses 4 to 8 times more energy than a thin client.[6] Another option to consider is a laptop rather than a desktop. Laptops consume approximately 5 times less energy than desktops.[7] Lastly, the use of an ENERGY STAR–rated LCD monitor will reduce energy consumption.

Ideally, desktops should use 4 watts of energy or less in sleep mode and 50 watts or less when idle. For laptops, the ideal is 2 watts or less in sleep mode and 14 to 22 watts or less in idle mode.[8] However, the EPA estimates that fewer than 10% of computers are set to use the sleep or hibernation mode.[9] This power-saving feature can easily be set up on your computer through the Control Panel's power options, although turning off your computer at the end of every workday is the best choice. Employees could also use a desktop device, such as EcoButton, to put the computer into sleep mode. Smart power strips can also conserve energy by turning off items after a period of inactivity. Smart strips are useful for printers, monitors, computers, and other items that can be powered down at the end of each day.

In addition to energy efficiency, green PCs are designed to contain fewer toxic materials (such as lead) in production and shipping and to contain more components that are made from recycled parts and that can again be recycled at the end of the machine's usefulness. The EPA's Electronic Product Environmental Assessment Tool allows you to compare computer models before making a purchase. See Table 7.1 for tips on how to be more environmentally friendly when printing from your desktop.

Table 7.1. Greener Printing From Your Computer

Before you print that next document, here are some ways you can achieve greener printing from your computer.

1.	**Make sure you are using an ENERGY STAR printer** (and computer). You may think this one's a no-brainer and you've got it covered, but wait . . . did you know that computer standards were revised in 2007 and new printer standards take effect this year? If your computer is older than 2007 and your printer is older than 2009, it may no longer meet ENERGY STAR standards, even though it met the standards that were in place at the time it was manufactured. If you should decide to upgrade, don't forget to recycle the old one!
2.	**Change the margins.** Studies at both Penn State University and Michigan State University found that changing margins can save paper. The Penn State study suggested that changing all university printer default margins to 0.75" (adding 19% more print space to the page) could save the university over $122,000 a year, and Michigan State estimated a savings of $67,512 a year.
3.	**Use paper with recycled content.** Although both the Penn State and Michigan State studies found that switching to recycled content paper was more expensive, this has not been the case in my consulting experience. Many businesses that are not under contractual purchasing agreements do have the flexibility to comparison shop. A recent client was able to save 10% on paper costs by switching from virgin fiber to recycled content paper. Other "green" options are to look for unbleached paper or, better yet, tree-free paper!
4.	**Recycle and buy recycled.** Recycle your paper, toner cartridges, and ink-jet cartridges. And don't forget to buy recycled, too!
5.	**Install software to manage and reduce paper usage.** Print management software programs (such as PaperCut, GreenPrint, and many others) can reduce printed pages and printer waste.
6.	**Use vegetable-based ink toner.** SoyPrint is an environmentally friendly alternative to petroleum-based toner. Look for additional vegetable-based toners and ink-jet cartridges to hit the market soon.
7.	**Change the font.** A Dutch company has created Ecofont, a new font that requires up to 20% less ink.[a] Ecofont is free to download and use.

By utilizing a combination of these suggestions, students at the University of Arkansas at Little Rock found that the College of Business could save 39% to 43% per year in paper and ink costs.[b] Above all, as your company upgrades computing equipment, seek out recycling centers or take-back programs for monitors, desktops, laptops, and other electronic items.

[a] Retrieved from http://www.ecofont.eu/english.html
[b] Barakovic et al., 2009.

E-Recycling

Many electronic items (monitors, computers, keyboards, televisions, external hardware devices, calculators, cell phones, and virtually anything that requires power for operation) can be donated to charitable organizations or repaired for continued use. For those electronics that cannot be repaired, electronics recycling (or e-cycling) is an option. The EPA[10] and Earth911 Web sites are the most comprehensive sources for finding where, what, and how to recycle in your local area. By donating unwanted electronics to charities or by recycling nonworking electronics, the sustainable business is doing its part to reduce electronics waste and divert it from the landfill.

Information Systems

In addition to the technology behind greening your computing operations, there are numerous software programs, or management information systems (MIS), to support corporate sustainability performance and to aid in executive decision-making tasks. MIS exist to measure any number of performance indicators related to social, environmental, and economic impact that are important to your company. Specific MIS can track carbon or greenhouse gas emissions (referred to as enterprise carbon accounting software), energy usage, compliance with voluntary and regulatory standards (such as ISO standards), environmental performance, supplier performance, or other sustainability indicators identified by your company. In addition to tracking sustainability-related performance indicators, software programs exist that are integrated with the Global Reporting Initiative (GRI) framework (see chapter 8) for ease in reporting sustainability performance.

Prior to selecting software programs, you should be clear on what principles, standards, measurement and accounting tools, reporting, assurance, and stakeholder engagement protocols the company is following (see chapter 8 and chapter 9). Your company should select an appropriate MIS that supports the corporate conduct standards it is pursuing, measures and tracks the indicators of those standards, provides accessible data, and allows ease of reporting data progress on the standards (see chapter 9). If the company does not subscribe to any particular voluntary or regulatory corporate conduct standards, the MIS should then meet the unique needs of the company for measurement, tracking, and reporting self-selected indicators.

An excellent resource for staying abreast of sustainability-related news in IT and information systems is Greener Computing. Other resources for computing professionals are Computer Professionals for Social Responsibility, the Green Grid, Climate Savers Computing Initiative, Green Computing Impact Organization, and the Green Electronics Council. For technology administrators, the Green ICT Strategies Course is free open-source courseware sponsored by the Australian Computer Society.

IT and MIS are both in a central position to help the organization reach its sustainability goals. That is, IT can help the organization operate in a more efficient and environmentally friendly manner, while MIS can serve an important role in transparency and gathering information for monitoring and reporting sustainability performance.

CHAPTER 8

Accounting

Accounting for the sustainable business extends beyond traditional financial and managerial accounting. Rather than externalizing the social and environmental costs of doing business, sustainability accounting seeks to honestly track, measure, and report direct and indirect economic, social, and environmental impacts of the business's operations. In other words, sustainability accounting seeks to internalize costs that have heretofore been externalized. Sustainability accounting may be known by other terms, such as social accounting, environmental accounting, social and environmental accounting, or social and ethical accounting, auditing, and reporting. Accounting specifically focused on greenhouse gas emissions is referred to as carbon accounting. Furthermore, reporting the results may be termed sustainability reporting, corporate social responsibility reporting, triple bottom line reporting, and nonfinancial reporting.

Prior to beginning any attempt to measure a company's triple bottom line impact, it should be clear what principles of corporate behavior the company aspires to follow and identify specific standards that support the principles.[1] Principles and standards will be discussed in greater detail in chapter 9, but it is important to understand that identification of principles and standards is a precursor to the selection of tracking, measuring, and reporting tools for sustainability accounting.

Since examining nonfinancial performance of the business is a voluntary initiative, a myriad of options have emerged for sustainability accounting, and the realm of possibilities can be quite overwhelming. In this chapter, we will focus only on areas specific to accounting (measurement and accounting tools, reporting, assurance, and stakeholder engagement) and will address senior-level management issues (principles and standards) in a later discussion (see chapter 9).

Measurement and Accounting Tools

There exists a plethora of measurement and accounting tools available, depending on the direction your company has decided to follow in terms of social impact, environmental impact, economic impact, or a complete three-dimensional approach to sustainability. Measurement and accounting tools refer to calculators and formulas and are not to be confused with standards, benchmarks, or thresholds for achievement (to be discussed in chapter 9). These measurement and accounting tools allow the company to measure its current behavior to establish a baseline, to set goals for improvement, and to measure future behavior to determine progress. This chapter will introduce you to the most common tools used by sustainable businesses.

Measuring Impact Tool

The World Business Council for Sustainable Development and the International Finance Corporation[2] have jointly created the Measuring Impact Tool. This tool offers the broadest three-dimensional sustainability coverage by measuring governance, (environmental) sustainability, assets, people, and financial flows. The Measuring Impact Tool is designed to work with the Global Reporting Initiative and the International Financial Corporation's Performance Standards for assessing projects on social and environmental standards before making investment decisions.

Greenhouse Gas Protocol

There are a number of other measurement and accounting tools focused only on the environmental dimension of sustainability. The Greenhouse Gas (GHG) Protocol was jointly created by the World Resources Institute and the World Business Council for Sustainability.[3] The GHG Protocol guides a company in creating base year measurements of GHG emissions, both direct and indirect, and allows the company to determine its own future goals for reduction. No comparative threshold or standard is provided. This tool can be used to implement the ISO 14064 standard on GHG emissions, and work currently underway will soon show how the GHG Protocol can be used with the Kyoto Protocol.

Although there are a plethora of online carbon calculators available to companies, they do not measure the full scope of emissions as detailed in the GHG Protocol.

Global Water Tool

The World Business Council for Sustainable Development's[4] Global Water Tool is currently under development with other groups around the world in order to standardize water footprint measurement, accounting, and reporting.

Global Environmental Management Initiative

In addition, the Global Environmental Management Initiative Water Tool,[5] while not a quantifiable measurement tool, offers a guide for the corporation in analyzing corporate water usage throughout the supply chain, determining water-related risks and opportunities, and determining if the business case exists to create a water strategy. Both of these water tools are related to a specific environmental focus on water usage and do not consider broader environmental impacts.

Life Cycle Assessments

Life cycle analyses (or assessments, LCAs) are another tool used to measure the environmental impact of a company's performance related to one specific product or service. LCAs do not assess the overall environmental performance of a company; they are focused only on the product or process under review. Nonetheless, LCA is a useful measurement tool for the sustainable business to help determine impacts of various products and services. Please refer to chapter 5 for further discussion on applications of LCA.

Reporting

The Global Reporting Initiative (GRI) is the world's most frequently used reporting guideline and format.[6] Currently in its third version, G3, this standard was used in reporting by nearly 1,500 businesses worldwide in 2007 and is becoming the accepted standard for reporting. The GRI is a template designed to be customized to the business; it offers industry-specific supplements to address the unique needs of the business. There are a number of software programs designed to aid in GRI reporting.

Assurance and Stakeholder Engagement

The final issues to consider in sustainability accounting are auditing and assurance as well as stakeholder engagement throughout the entire process. Sometimes referred to as a social (or environmental) audit, an ethical audit, or monitoring, auditing and assurance allows verification that proper checks and balances are in place to support the claims of the organization. There are currently two general assurance standards available, the AA1000 Assurance Standard and the International Standard on Assurance Engagements (ISAE) 3000, and one stakeholder engagement standard, AA1000 Stakeholder Engagement Standard.

AA1000 Assurance Standard

AccountAbility's[7] AA1000 Assurance Standard seeks to create a process for implementation and reporting of the AA1000 Framework. To ensure consistency in implementing the assurance standards, AccountAbility offers certification courses to become a Sustainability Assurance Practitioner.

International Standard on Assurance Engagements 3000

As another option, the International Auditing and Assurance Standards Board of the International Federation of Accountants[8] has put forth the International Standard on Assurance Engagements (ISAE) 3000 standards for auditing nonfinancial statements. Keeping in mind that sustainability accounting is optional in the United States, some organizations may opt for providing internal assurance of activities and reporting. However, to increase credibility, organizations should opt for external third-party assurance from independent boards or firms providing sustainability audits or related services.

AA1000 Stakeholder Engagement Standard

Stakeholder engagement is another critical element that must be implemented throughout the entire sustainability accounting process. Stakeholder engagement is a process to promote cooperation between the organization and all its stakeholders as a means to involve and respond to the interests of stakeholders. AccountAbility[9] has issued the AA1000 Stakeholder Engagement Standard; however, it appears that most organizations develop their own stakeholder engagement process.

Accounting Methods

In recent years, overhead costs have become an increasingly significant part of product cost. Managers need high quality cost information to maintain greater control of processes and achieve quicker responses to competitive pressures. As a result, firms are using activity-based costing (ABC) to pinpoint internal company costs associated with each step in a production or service-related activity.[10] While ABC is appropriate for financial reporting according to Generally Accepted Accounting Principles (GAAP), sustainable businesses seek to account for all costs over the long term. That is, sustainable businesses are looking beyond internal costs and are including broader considerations such as costs associated with the entire value chain or, as discussed in past chapters, the costs associated with cradle to cradle activities. Sustainability costing seeks to internalize those costs that have been historically externalized. The sustainable business now considers the financial costs of products and services over their lifetime and throughout the supply chain rather than passing those costs to society and the environment.

Accounting methods taking a longer term orientation include life cycle costing, life cycle environmental cost analysis, and full cost accounting. Life cycle costing (LCC) or life cycle cost analysis seeks to fully capture and internalize costs by examining the total cost from inception costs of products (development or purchase, delivery, installation) to operating costs (energy, water, maintenance, and repair) to end-of-life costs of products (removal, replacement, salvage, disposal).[11] LCC cannot be used for financial reporting and, in general, is not consistent with GAAP, but is a useful tool for managers in costing from a planning standpoint.

Life cycle environmental cost analysis (LCECA) is another form of LCC; however, the objective of LCECA is to include eco-costs into the total costs of the product, or the direct and indirect costs of the environmental impacts caused by the product. With LCECA, sustainable businesses can more clearly identify feasible alternatives for cost-effective, environmental products.[12]

Full-cost accounting (FCA), also known as total cost accounting, broadens the assessment of external costs and incorporates future costs. This approach seeks to determine the full cost of the societal, economic, and environmental impact (triple bottom line) of a given manufacturing or service activity. Fundamental to FCA is the valuation of the opportunity costs, hidden costs, or trade-offs that were made when the option to use a particular limited resource was selected.[13]

Accounting professionals are in a unique position to help the organization accurately measure and report social, economic, and environmental impacts. Various accounting methods and measurement and accounting tools aid in capturing the real costs of products and processes. Furthermore, a common sustainability-reporting framework exists to guide organizations in understanding what items to report. Lastly, guidelines for assurance and stakeholder engagement also exist to provide assistance for businesses.

CHAPTER 9

Next Steps: Sustainability Strategy

So where do you go from here? By now, it should be apparent that sustainability infiltrates every aspect of the business. Although individuals may champion sustainability initiatives at various points throughout the organization, a sustainable business incorporates sustainability into every aspect of the firm; sustainability becomes central to the overall direction and strategy of the firm. That is, one can never actually pursue the goal of a sustainable business without integrating sustainability into the fabric of the organization's strategic direction. Sustainability is recognized as being more than an initiative, a program, or an activity; it is recognized as a new worldview or mindset regarding how business operates. This requires commitment and buy-in by those in top positions who are responsible for the overall management of the company. But what if your company's senior executives are not yet convinced that sustainability is a worthwhile pursuit?

Sustainability as Incremental Improvements

It is not unusual for sustainability to be championed by one person, department, or division. If this is the case in your company, we applaud you for your initiative and foresight! Or perhaps there has not yet been any particular sustainability emphasis within your company and you wonder where to start. As such, we make these suggestions:

1. **Prove the business case**. Start with a small project in your division or department. Over time, refine the project so that it can be scaled and transferred to other areas of the company. Above all, make the business case by calculating the positive impacts and

results of the project (often quantified in terms of savings, other improvements, or both).

2. **Establish a green team**. A green team can explore options for sustainability and identify the low-hanging fruit (easy-to-implement projects that are low cost but offer high returns). Work with others who share your vision for a sustainable workplace.

3. **Raise awareness**. Education and awareness are critical for change. Use a newsletter, Web site, discussion group, bulletin board, or other means of communication to publicize successes and educate others on sustainability impacts. One thing we have learned is that you must show people how sustainability (and its impacts) relates to them.

If your company has moved beyond the stage of sustainability as incremental improvements, then your company is well on its way toward embracing sustainability as strategy. We devote the rest of this chapter to a discussion of how sustainability is deeply embedded throughout the organization as a strategic priority of the company.

Sustainability as Strategy

Sustainability as strategy will encompass all aspects of the company's operations, as demonstrated in the previous chapters. Sustainability as strategy entails a new perspective, recognizing that financial gain is not the only imperative of the firm. Rather, social, environmental, and economic gains can be enjoyed by all and business is the vehicle through which it can happen. Your business can be used to make the world a better place. This idea gains much resistance from those who have been trained to believe that profit is the only purpose of business. That is, some may balk at the idea that a business has any responsibility beyond that to its shareholders.[1] For those sharing this perspective, consider the future risks inherent in current operational practices if more stringent social, environmental, or economic regulations emerge. Every executive and Board of Directors should be attuned to world trends impacting the global business environment[2] and conduct a risk audit of current operations (and the supply chain) to identify vulnerabilities in light of these global trends. A risk audit would entail an honest evaluation of energy usage, water usage, waste produced, toxins used or produced (or both), human resources practices, value and supply chain operations, community relations, regulations and standards, customer relations, technology, and the like. Furthermore, an honest assessment of strengths, weaknesses, opportunities, and threats is in order. The progressive company will view potential risks as opportunities to improve the organization and to seize new market opportunities. In the words of Peter Drucker, "Every single social and global issue of our day is a business opportunity in disguise."[3]

Many successful businesses are exemplars of sustainable and responsible business practices; some before it was "fashionable." Classic examples include Ben & Jerry's (now owned by Unilever), Whole Foods Market, Body Shop (now owned by L'Oréal), ShoreBank, Interface, Newman's Own, Burt's Bees, Seventh Generation, Tom's of Maine (now owned by Colgate), Greyston Bakery, Green Mountain Coffee Roasters, Armstrong International, Virgin Group, Golden Temple, and many others. Today we see a new generation of companies continuing and even expanding on sustainable and responsible business models. A brief overview of a very small selection of these companies is provided in part II of this book, "Sustainable Business: Case Examples." These companies serve as role models for others pursuing sustainability.

While many businesses will forge their own path toward sustainability, there is a growing infrastructure of principles and standards to help guide and provide direction to companies. Adoption of these principles and standards is voluntary, allowing businesses the flexibility to choose among the many options available. We will discuss the most commonly adopted principles and standards.

Principles of Corporate Conduct

There currently exists a growing body of protocols for businesses that seek to be sustainable. In addition to creating a strong values-based and ethical corporate culture, many businesses will explore the numerous principles for corporate behavior. Principles of corporate behavior are broad sweeping guidelines to which the business subscribes and which reflect the values and goals of the business. Companies will select one or more that are most appropriate to the type of business and that reflects the outcomes the business wishes to achieve. Whether or not the business elects to become an official signatory of the principles, they can still offer guidance on the type of values the corporation will seek to uphold. We will briefly explain the most common principles for corporate behavior.

United Nations Global Compact. Among the most commonly referenced set of principles for corporate conduct is the United Nations Global Compact. The UN Global Compact contains 10 principles for responsible and sustainable business activity in the areas of human rights, labor, the environment, and anticorruption. Over 4,700 businesses worldwide have become signatories (participation is also open to nonprofits, academic institutions, and municipalities).[4] The UN Global Compact is the business extension of broader UN goals, including the UN Millennium Development Goals (MDG) for governments and international organizations. The UN MDG set forth eight goals (with 21 accompanying targets) related to poverty, education, gender equality, child mortality, maternal health, disease, the environment, and global partnerships. The MDG initiative has been signed by 189 UN member states and international organizations with the goal of achievement by 2015.

AA1000 Framework. Another popular set of principles for corporate conduct is the AccountAbility 1000 (AA1000) series. The AA1000 Framework seeks to engage all stakeholders in determining the organization's course toward its vision. The AA1000 Framework is designed to complement the Global Reporting Initiative (GRI), the most frequently used sustainability reporting framework worldwide (discussed in chapter 8).

Caux Round Table Principles. The Caux Round Table Principles provide a global vision for business conduct based upon shared values. The principles were developed in 1994 and offer a self-assessment and improvement process self-appraisal tool for organizations to assess their progress.

ISO 26000. Currently under development are the International Standards Organization's (ISO) 26000 guidelines. The ISO's 26000 standards are expected to be released in 2010 and will serve as a set of principles or guidelines on corporate responsibility, or the relationship between a business and all its stakeholders. The new ISO 26000 standards will serve as guidelines only and will not become part of the ISO certification process.

The Natural Step. The Natural Step puts forth four broad beliefs or philosophies on how business should operate within the natural environment.

For those who subscribe to these value statements, the Natural Step offers a framework and tools to assist businesses.

The Aspen Principles. The Aspen Institute's Business and Society Program provides educators and executives with research, information, and opportunities for sustainability and values-based leadership. The Aspen Institute's Business and Society Program has put forth the Aspen Principles. These principles suggest that a long-term focus will ultimately lead to value creation for the corporation. Specifically, they promote improved corporate governance as a means toward long-term value creation for the company, economic growth for the nation, and better service to society.

Coalition of Environmentally Responsible Economies Principles. For the business that chooses to focus only on environmental impact, the Coalition of Environmentally Responsible Economies (CERES) Principles focus on the environment and climate change.

There are a number of less frequently used principles for corporate conduct. These include the defunct UN Human Rights Norms for Business, the Organization for Economic Cooperation and Development Principles of Corporate Governance and Guidelines for Multinational Enterprises, the International Chamber of Commerce Business Charter for Sustainable Development, and the Global Sullivan Principles of Social Responsibility.

Standards

After determining the principles to which a business will subscribe, the next step is to select standards for performance. Some standards identify specific guidelines for corporate behavior while others detail specific quantifiable benchmarks to achieve. There have been efforts to create uniform standards that apply to all organizations and all industries; these have had mixed success. Uniform standards include the Sustainability-Integrated Guidelines for Management, or SIGMA Project, Certified B Corporations, the Corporate Responsibility Index, and the now defunct Social Venture Network Standards of Corporate Responsibility. In addition, there are a growing number of local, regional, and national organizations that identify required criteria to become certified as a sustainable or green business (e.g., Bay Area Green Business Program).

SIGMA Project. Project SIGMA offers guidelines for companies on social, environmental, and economic performance. The guidelines attempt to integrate five types of capital (human, financial, social, manufactured, and natural) while practicing accountability and transparency with all stakeholders.

Certified B Corporations. B corporations are a new type of corporation. To be certified as a B corporation requires companies to (a) meet comprehensive and transparent social and environmental performance standards, (b) amend governance documents to incorporate the interests of all stakeholders, and (c) build collective voice through the power of a unifying brand.

Corporate Responsibility Index. Business in the Community's Corporate Responsibility Index is an online survey of participating companies' performance in seven areas of corporate responsibility: strategy, integration, management, social impact, environmental impact, assurance, and disclosure. The annual results are compiled to create a benchmark of corporate responsibility. Participating companies receive a personalized report to compare their own practices to the average benchmark. This process highlights the gap between current performance and the industry benchmark.

Not all standards address the full three-dimensional realm of sustainability. Some standards focus only on the social or environmental performance of an organization; other standards apply only to a particular industry.

Standards for Social Performance. Standards with a more narrow focus on socially related concerns include ISO 9000 (labor standards), SA 8000 (labor standards), Ethical Trading Initiative (ETI, labor standards), OHSAS 18001 (occupational health and safety), FairTrade (agriculture and handicrafts from emerging economies), and the Standards of Excellence in corporate community involvement (corporate citizenship).

Standards for Environmental Performance. Standards with a more narrow focus on environmentally related concerns include ISO 14000, the Kyoto Protocol, LEED (Leadership in Energy and Environmental Design) certification from the U.S. Green Building Council, and the Forest Stewardship Council. In addition, there is explosive growth in the number of local, regional, and national organizations offering certification as a green business.

Standards for Industry Performance. Standards with a focus on a particular industry are too numerous to mention and exist for every known industry. However, among the more well-known industry standards are the Apparel Industries Partnership (apparel), Fair Labor Association (apparel), Common Codes for the Coffee Community (coffee), Responsible Care (chemicals), Extractive Industries Transparency Initiative (mining, oil, gas, etc.), Green Computing Maturity Model Process (computing), RugMark (handwoven rugs), Equator Principles (banking and finance), and the AIChE Sustainablity Index (engineering and scientific firms), just to mention a few.

While adoption of principles and standards are neither required nor necessary for sustainability, they do add credibility to the organization's sustainability efforts. Upon determining principles for corporate conduct and specific standards to follow, the sustainable business turns to the task of implementing the sustainability strategy throughout the various functional areas of the company and tracking and measuring sustainability performance (as explained in each of the preceding chapters).

Making the Sustainability Commitment

As a strategy, sustainability requires leadership and top-level commitment, strong values and ethics deeply embedded in the corporate culture, and incorporation throughout all business activities. Sustainability must be embedded in the core competencies and competitive position of the company and engage all stakeholders. Finally, reexamination of the business model, organizational structure, reward system, and other management systems are in order. We will examine each of these in further detail.

Leadership and Top-Level Commitment

Sustainability requires commitment by the Board of Directors, CEO, and top management team. This commitment and leadership begins at an executive level and is spread throughout the organization. Leadership and top-level commitment demonstrate that sustainability is a priority for the organization. Many corporations have created new positions, such as Corporate Responsibility Officer or Corporate Sustainability Officer, to oversee this aspect of company operations.

In addition to supporting sustainability as a value of the organization, many organizations, such as the U.S. Green Building Council, have turned to dynamic governance (also termed sociocracy)[5] as a model for corporate governance, decision making, and organizational structure. The sociocratic model has four principles: decisions are made by consent, the organization is a hierarchy of semiautonomous circles, circles are double-linked with two representatives from each circle serving on the next circle up in the hierarchy, and elections are held by consent. The model is inclusive, gives everyone a voice, and reaches consensus easier and faster than traditional governance, decision making, or organizational structure models.

Values and Ethics

One thing we see in common throughout sustainable organizations is a strong values-based and ethical corporate culture. In fact, it is argued that the strategic deployment of corporate values is a necessary building block for competitive advantage in this new era of sustainable business.[6] Training and development opportunities for employees will focus on personal growth and development, instilling corporate values and ethics, and promoting sustainability.[7]

Core Competencies and Competitive Position

As we have seen throughout this book, sustainability encompasses the entire organization. Sustainability is deeply integrated throughout all activities, functions, operations, and business activities. Sustainability should also be deeply embedded in the company's core competencies[8] and contribute to a strong competitive position for the company. That is, your business must develop strengths, competencies, and expertise in a way that sets it apart from its competitors (which makes the business unique, one-of-a-kind, and different) and that produces a result that is valued by customers.[9] The business must develop a skill set that promotes its core competencies and strengthens its competitive position so that the business becomes known as the place to patronize for those who seek out that particular core competence.

As an example, if you think of a business that has the absolute lowest prices, one particular business may come to mind. Or if you think of a business that has combined low prices and stylish or trendy items, another particular business may come to mind. These descriptions might identify the particular business's core competency (or what they are known for, the business's area of expertise). It is also certain that a broad skill set has been developed across all functions and dimensions of the business to promote and advance the core competency, thereby strengthening its competitive position in the market place.

A sustainable business must identify its core competency (what it is known for), identify the set of skills across the entire range of business functions that must be developed in order to perfect the core competency, and use this information to strengthen its competitive position against rivals. Sustainability must be rooted in the core competencies and must contribute to strengthening the company's competitive position; sustainability should be the linchpin of, rather than peripheral to, the company's strategy.

Stakeholder Engagement and Assurance

Sustainability requires a shift in mindset in the way companies interact with stakeholders. Companies have historically viewed stakeholders in terms of their threat and power and have developed strategies for managing stakeholders in order to reduce their threat and neutralize their power.[10] By contrast, a sustainable business will interact with stakeholders, including critics, listen to their concerns, and will seek to engage them in identifying plausible solutions. There appears to be no prominently used stakeholder engagement standard although several exist, including AA1000 Stakeholder Engagement Standard and the SIGMA Project's Stakeholder Engagement Tool (both discussed in chapter 8). It appears that most companies develop their own approach to stakeholder engagement. As such, companies must consider how each stakeholder will be impacted within the sustainability efforts.

Suppliers. A commitment to sustainability will require that the company engage its suppliers in the move toward more sustainable business practices. This will require a critical analysis of suppliers' current social, environmental, and economic impacts. It is of critical importance to engage suppliers in your transition toward sustainability so that your business has a complete understanding of the supplies being used, the conditions under which they were produced, and their associated impacts. Sustainable businesses often work with suppliers to help them become more sustainable. Furthermore, suppliers need to understand what types of products and services you seek to support your sustainability strategy.

Customers. Customers can offer valuable insights regarding your business and should be engaged in sustainability efforts. In addition, customers should be part of the sustainable business's education and communication efforts related to sustainability. This group of stakeholders might ultimately be affected by changes in product or service offerings.

Employees. Employees can be engaged in the sustainability process in a number of ways. Training and education will be critical (as discussed in chapter 3). For example, employees must understand their role in the sustainability strategy, rewards for achieving sustainability goals, and the change in corporate emphasis from a profit orientation to a more balanced triple bottom line orientation. Employees must also frequently receive communications related to sustainability progress. Lastly, employees can be an invaluable source of sustainability-related innovations.

Shareholders. Shareholders must also understand the change in corporate emphasis from profit orientation to triple bottom line. Studies show that sustainability-focused companies outperform other companies. Most recently, a study of companies with a commitment to sustainability showed that they continued to outperform other companies even during the midst of the economic crisis during the period of May through November 2008.[11]

Society. Communities and society at large are important stakeholders that must be included in a company's sustainability efforts. Americans are skeptical of and generally do not trust businesses, particularly big businesses.[12] Furthermore, it may be more difficult to overcome image and reputation problems.

As we discuss society as a stakeholder, globalization and international strategies bear mention here. Once a company begins conducting business outside its own borders, the sustainable business will become cognizant of the unintended consequences of traditional international strategies.[13] Companies have been accused of exploiting human and natural resources in areas in which they have business operations.

Base of the pyramid (BOP) strategies seek to address these concerns and improve the social, environmental, and economic performance of corporations conducting business in emerging economies.[14] Not without criticism,[15] BOP strategies are an effort to adopt localized nonethnocentric partnership-based approaches to conducting business in emerging markets. BOP strategies also seek social, environmental, and economic benefits for all partners involved. The Base of the Pyramid Protocol 2.0[16] provides an excellent standard for conducting business in emerging economies.

One example of a BOP strategy is Grameen Bank. Muhammad Yunus started Grameen Bank as a means of providing credit to the poorest residents in rural India. Loans are made to an individual, without collateral, whose family and friends guarantee the loan. Loans are typically small, or microloans, but can make a significant impact in residents' quality of life. Yunus was awarded the Nobel Peace Prize in 2006 for this social banking model and strategy that ultimately fights poverty and promotes self-sufficiency in BOP communities.

Other stakeholders. The list of a company's potential stakeholders is much larger than the five groups of stakeholders mentioned here. Other possible stakeholders include creditors, environmental organizations, nonprofits, government, and many more. The sustainable organization will engage each group in a cooperative dialogue to generate mutual benefit.

Numerous academic centers, research centers, and nonprofit organizations around the world work with businesses toward a sustainable future. Among those centers and organizations are the Applied Sustainability Center, Business Alliance for Local Living Economies, Center for Business as an Agent of World Benefit, Center for Companies That Care, Center for Corporate Citizenship, Center for Responsible Business, Center for Sustainable Business Practices, Center for Sustainable Enterprise, Center for Sustainable Global Enterprise, Consortium on Green Design and Manufacturing, Enterprise for a Sustainable World, Erb Institute for Sustainable Global Enterprise, Ethical Trading Initiative, Forum for Corporate Sustainability Management, Global Institute of Sustainability, Green Design Institute, Minnesota Center for Corporate Responsibility, National Association of Socially Responsible Organizations, Peace Through Commerce, World Business Council for Sustainable Development, and World Resources Institute. Sustainable businesses recognize the importance of mutual learning and networking with others in order to generate a shared knowledge base.

Assurance. It is important to provide assurance (a social audit, ethical audit, or monitoring) that systems are in place to track and measure sustainability claims made by a company. There are two widely used assurance standards that companies will want to consider: AccountAbility's AA1000 Assurance Standard 2008 and the International Auditing and Assurance Standards Board's International Standard for Assurance Engagements (ISAE 3000). Both are discussed in detail in chapter 8.

Business Model, Systems, and Structure

Incorporating sustainability throughout all functional areas of the business and across the entire supply chain of the business will require closer examination of the business model being used, the various management systems in place (including reward systems), and the organizational design or structure in place; changes may be in order. A business model is the way in which a company's value chain is organized in order to be most efficient and effective in achieving its social, environmental, and economic goals while making a profit.

A particular example of an innovative business model emerging in this era of sustainable business is a social or open business model that engages stakeholders in determining and defining how the business will operate. Stakeholders are the decision makers and contribute to the ongoing operations of the business. First termed crowdsourcing,[17] social business models leverage the power of mass collaboration in creating a successful business.[18] One example of a successful social business model is the sports apparel company nvohk where anyone can become a partner for $50. Partners contribute apparel and logo designs, vote on designs, vote on advertising, sponsorships, and which charities receive 10% of the company profits, and make many other company-related decisions.

Furthermore, the company may need to reexamine its management and control systems (including corporate governance and reward systems), organizational structure, corporate culture, and other aspects of the business (such as the discussion on dynamic governance earlier in this chapter). For example, as with all aspects of strategy and strategic planning, the company must set sustainability-related goals, measure results, train, educate, and involve employees and other stakeholders, and tie rewards to the achievement of goals. The organizational hierarchy in place must be one that supports the sustainability-related goals and objectives of the strategic plan. Sustainability is well planned and coordinated across all activities of the corporation, and the business model, systems, and structure must support the sustainability-related goals of the strategic plan.

Conclusion

We have presented an enormous amount of information throughout this book that may appear overwhelming. At this point you are probably wondering where to begin. First, keep in mind that there is no easy one-step approach to becoming sustainable; sustainability is a *continuous* process that requires critical self-analysis, honesty, innovation, and risk. That is, before beginning this journey toward sustainability, a business should be prepared to be self-reflective, critical, and honest about all its operations and associated impacts, and a business should be ready to take risks and be innovative, moving beyond its comfort zone, or business as usual.

Second, consider that sustainability encompasses the operations of the entire business: every process, every activity, and every function. A business will not be able to implement one or a few changes and proclaim that the business has achieved sustainability. A business should be prepared to apply the aforementioned critical self-analysis, honesty, innovation, and risk across all processes, all activities, and every function of the business. Sustainability is a company-wide change in mindset, philosophy, views, and practices related to how the business operates.

Lastly, realize that sustainability incorporates a triple bottom line in evaluating company performance: the environmental, social, and economic impact of the business (also referred to as planet, people, and profit). Since pursuit of this triple bottom line is central to sustainability, our discussion on this point bears repeating.

The efforts that a business makes to reduce its environmental impact are equated with the term going green. Since green modifications can often be translated into financial terms (cost, return on investment, savings), this is often the first step a business will pursue in beginning the sustainability journey. Among some of the commonly implemented activities here are creating company "green teams" to explore and champion ways to become more environmentally friendly, recycling and reducing waste, using recycled products, changing to compact fluorescent lightbulbs and retrofitting other lighting, implementing energy-saving activities, pursuing LEED certification, and implementing ISO 14001 standards.

The efforts that a business makes to increase its social impact often refer to the impact of company policies, procedures, practices, and operations on employees, on those employed by its suppliers, and on communities, cultures, and society. A business should critically evaluate the impact of its own practices and policies on employees. A business should also demand transparency from suppliers to understand where all supplies were generated and the conditions under which they were produced. Common activities of a sustainable business include the use of Fair Trade products (such as coffee in the break room), avoidance of products that may have been made with child or forced labor, contributions to solving social problems, implementation of SA 8000 standards, providing fair and safe working conditions, living wages, insurance and other benefits, and a offering employees a work–life balance.

The efforts that a business makes to maximize its economic impact often refer to the economic impact the business has on communities or societies within which it operates. This does not refer to the "profit" the company shows on financial statements but rather refers to how the community or society "profits" from the presence of the business, which, in turn, will result in continued profitability for the company. That is, economic impact refers to the continued prosperity of the business due to the economic benefit it provides to the community or society. Common activities include the payment of fair and living wages, providing positive impacts on the local economy and on local economic development (job creation, tax dollars, property values), and assessing the stress or relief created for local public service systems as a result of the business's operations.

So how can your business become a sustainable business? To begin your journey, we recommend that you pick one thing, one process, one activity, or one department. Be prepared to apply critical self-analysis and be honest in identifying the associated environmental, social, and economic impact of current business practices, processes, and operations. Begin by measuring the current impact, set goals and timelines for improvement, and then track and measure those improvements and results. Do not be afraid to experiment and learn what other companies are doing. Involve and listen to employees, suppliers, customers, and others, including critics.

As your company begins its sustainability journey, remember that changes will impact operations company-wide. Therefore, sustainability education is important for employees, suppliers, and customers alike, as is communication of progress toward sustainability goals. It is also important not to overstate claims or accomplishments (referred to as greenwashing). Yet another word of caution is to remember that sustainability is three-dimensional. While the concept of green is becoming mainstream, sustainability requires that you not overlook the other areas of impact (social and economic impacts). As a company begins to build a track record of changes and successes, continue bringing more processes, activities, and departments into the fold until the entire organization is focused on the triple bottom line of sustainability. Above all, remember that as a company pursues sustainability, there is no end to this journey; it is a continuous process and refinement of the way we view business within the context of society. Refer to Table 9.1 for additional tips.

We return to our definition introduced at the beginning of the book: a sustainable business is *one that operates in the interest of all current and future stakeholders in a manner that ensures the long-term health and survival of the business and its associated economic, social, and environmental systems.* Sustainability requires a new view of business and a new philosophy on how business should be conducted. Armed with this new perspective, we believe that business can become a vehicle for positive change.

Table 9.1. How to Begin the Journey Toward Sustainability

1.	Educate, inform, and engage stakeholders.
2.	Pick one thing (one process, one activity, or one department).
3.	Identify and measure its associated environmental, social, and economic impact as a result of current business practices, processes, and operations.
4.	Engage stakeholders in identifying areas for improvement, creating measurable goals, and setting timelines for achievement.
5.	Assign specific tasks and responsibilities.
6.	Track, measure, and document results.
7.	Refine and adjust as needed.
8.	Communicate progress.
9.	Expand efforts to other processes, activities, and departments (and repeat the previous steps).
10.	Share your knowledge; mentor others.

PART II

Sustainable Business: Case Examples

Now that you are familiar with the concept of sustainable business and how it impacts every aspect of the business, we are delighted to turn to real case examples of sustainable business practices. Fortunately, there are an increasing number of businesses moving toward sustainability. While the examples are too numerous to list here, we have selected a small sample of for-profit entities that are striving to maximize social, environmental, and economic impacts. Although space prohibits us from providing an in-depth look at each company, we have briefly highlighted some of the unique contributions each is making toward sustainability.

These case examples showcase the wide array of approaches being used by businesses of varying sizes in various industries. Some of these companies are making gains in one of the dimensions of sustainability (social, environmental, economic); others have a fully developed three-dimensional approach to sustainability. But what each of these case examples has in common is that they demonstrate it is possible to successfully pursue sustainability and a triple bottom line. You need look no further than the following companies for proof of those who exemplify our own motto: "Make a Profit, Make an Impact, Make a Difference. Because Sustainable Business is Good Business."©

Alaffia Sustainable Skin Care[1]

Alaffia Sustainable Skin Care (Olympia, Washington) is the North American retail and wholesale distributor of Fair Trade shea butter, African black soap, and tropical oils from the Alaffia/Agbanga Karite Cooperative in Togo, Africa.

The company follows a triple bottom line approach (people, profit, and planet). Alaffia's relationship with the Cooperative brings income to and empowers communities in Togo. Additionally, Alaffia and Agbanga Karite donate 10% of sales proceeds (or 30% of income, whichever is greater) to community empowerment projects, AIDS and malaria outreach, and educational scholarships in Togo.

Alaffia sponsors Bicycles for Education, donates school supplies and uniforms, funds reforestation projects, and started the Alaffia Women's Clinic in Togo. Alaffia also provides scholarships to Washington state students, donates soap and lotion to women's shelters, offers Fair Trade talks, tours of the Washington facility, and community outreach and education on Fair Trade. With the help of others, the nonprofit Global Alliance for Community Empowerment (GACE) was formed to oversee community projects that focus on self-empowerment, the advancement of fair trade, education, sustainable living, and gender equality in Togo.

Through work individually and with GACE, Agbanga Karite Cooperative has provided more than 300 children with books, uniforms, and supplies for the 2004–2005 school year; paid the school enrollment fees for these children; donated desks and chairs to a local primary school in the village of Adjorogo; and donated and installed new school roofs on rural schools in central Togo.

baabaaZuZu[2]

baabaaZuZu (Lake Leelanau, Michigan) makes clothing from items that would otherwise be discarded. All clothing is made from 100% recycled materials, primarily wool and tweed. Most of the supply comes from secondhand shops. Each product is unique, but they all have a common pocket and hand-sewn blanket stitch. The product line consists of jackets, vests, hats, scarves, mittens, purses and bags, pins, and Christmas stockings.

Better World Club[3]

Better World Club (Portland, Oregon) is a nationwide auto and travel club. An alternative to other auto and travel clubs, the Better World Club provides emergency roadside assistance, travel planning services (auto, flight, and hotel), maps, trip routing services, partnership discounts, and auto insurance.

In addition to the standard fare for auto and travel clubs, the Better World Club also offers bicycle roadside assistance, discounts on hybrid or biodiesel auto rentals, discounts at eco-lodging facilities, discounts on eco-tours, membership discounts for hybrid vehicle owners, an online carbon emissions calculator, carbon offsets for your auto or travel plans, and a donation of 1% of revenue to environmental cleanup efforts and advocacy.

BetterWorld Telecom[4]

BetterWorld Telecom (Reston, Virginia) is a telecommunications company providing voice and data solutions for businesses and organizations with social and sustainable missions. The company donates 3% of revenues (administered by the BetterWorld Charitable Foundation) to nonprofit organizations through grants that help children, education, fair trade, and the environment. The company's goal is to donate $1 million per year by 2012.

BetterWorld Telecom is striving for a paperless operation. When paper usage is necessary, it is 100% recycled or tree-free kenaf paper. The company is also carbon-neutral.

Boulevard Bread Company[5]

Boulevard Bread Company (Little Rock, Arkansas) is a multisite restaurant committed to being a low-impact and environmentally friendly business. The company buys organic produce from local sources when possible. The company uses biodegradable and compostable disposable utensils and cups made from corn or potato by-products. Carry-out containers that are not compostable are recyclable. Boulevard Bread sells only 100% Fair Trade and organic coffee, uses earth-friendly cleaners, uses recycled paper products, and recycles glass, cardboard, aluminum, and plastics. The company is pursuing zero waste. All locations have been retrofitted with energy-efficient lighting, and the main site has installed a tankless water heater.

Boulevard Bread Company recently joined forces with other local restaurants to create the Green Restaurant Alliance to network and support area restaurants pursuing environmentally friendly operations. In addition, Boulevard Bread supports the community through charitable donations, collaboration, local sustainable agriculture, and through training and mentoring other green food businesses.

Boutique Mix[6]

Boutique Mix (Washington, DC) is a fashion boutique offering "An International Ethnik Chik Kollection" of unique items from around the world. Boutique Mix sources natural organic handmade items following Fair Trade principles and nonhandmade items that are organic and use low-impact dyes and processes. Boutique Mix also offers its own line of Miatta-MiMi jewelry and gift baskets using beads and other accessories collected around the world.

An incredible 25% of all profits go toward charitable causes. Thirty-five percent of the charitable proceeds go toward rebuilding Sierra Leone by providing school supplies and other necessities to needy children, another 35% goes toward sponsoring children around the world through Plan USA, Children International, St. Jude's Children's Hospital, and the Christian Children's Fund. The remaining 30% of charitable proceeds go toward Kiva loans for entrepreneurs in developing countries and to the Rebuilding Sierra Leone One Child at a Time campaign.

Brilliant Earth[7]

Brilliant Earth (San Francisco, California) specializes in conflict-free diamond jewelry. The conflict-free diamonds are from Canadian mines that follow the country's environmental laws, the most rigorous in the world. Sapphires used in Brilliant Earth jewelry are sourced from Australia or Malawi following Fair Trade principles. When possible, gold and platinum are reclaimed through recycled jewelry and industrial waste. Brilliant Earth dedicates 5% of profits to the nonprofit organizations Green Diamonds and MedShare International to support African communities negatively affected by the diamond trade industry.

Burgerville[8]

Burgerville (Vancouver, Washington) is a chain of 39 Pacific Northwest quick-service restaurants offering seasonal organic, local, and healthy food. In addition, they use hormone-free milk, and kid's meals come with safe and educational toys, such as biodegradable garden pots and vegetable seed packets. Burgerville purchases 100% of their energy usage with wind power credits, they recycle used canola oil into biodiesel, and they offer affordable health care to employees. They are working toward all 39 restaurants becoming fully recycling and composting.

Caracalla[9]

Caracalla (Little Rock, Arkansas) is a salon and day spa with an aggressive recycling program that extends beyond the typical recycling of waste. Some of the unique ways in which Caracalla supports the reduce, reuse, recycle mantra are to buy reclaimed items for retail sale (such as mittens and hats made from old discarded sweaters), they sell vintage items, they recycle cut hair by sending it to Matter of Trust to be woven into hair mats capable of absorbing chemical oil spills, and they recycle worn pantyhose and stockings with Matter of Trust for the same purpose. In addition, the company purchases and sells recycled items, such as paper, bags, office supplies, toilet tissue, hand towels, pet toys, and even biodegradable bags for picking up dog waste. The salon is decorated with reclaimed and vintage items and uses or sells eco-friendly products, such as homemade herbal wraps (no packaging waste!), bamboo hairbrushes, hemp bags, natural hair and body products, soy candles in recycled glass jars, efficient lighting, and reusable coffee mugs.

Caracalla supports the local economy by purchasing from local and organic suppliers, particularly other sustainable or green businesses, and buys in bulk to reduce packaging waste.

The company also supports the local community through charitable donations and by offering free haircuts to customers who are donating hair to charity.

Clean Air Lawn Care[10]

Clean Air Lawn Care (Fort Collins, Colorado) uses solar-powered lawn mowers for yard care. Trucks are equipped with solar panels to recharge the mowers throughout the day. When it is not possible to use solar-powered mowers, the company uses conventional mowers fueled with biodiesel. Clean Air Lawn Care will also remove yard waste to an organic waste recycling center, where available. The company purchases carbon offsets for the business and is carbon neutral. On the company Web site, you will find an online calculator to determine the carbon emissions of your current mowing methods. You will also find a scholarship application for environmentally minded students preparing to enroll in college for the first time.

Clean Green Collision[11]

At Clean Green Collision (Oakland, California) precautions are taken during auto repair to ensure that dust, remnants, and hazardous chemicals do not enter the car and leave odors and fumes that could potentially harm customers. Filtration is an important part of Clean Green Collision's eco-friendly approach: paint fumes and other emissions are filtered, air in the sanding area is filtered twice, and there is a filtration system to capture emissions from welding. Other eco-friendly efforts include photosynthesis curing, use of water-based paints, remodeling with recycled and reclaimed windows and doors, and use of local suppliers. The shop claims it currently creates only 30%–40% of the emissions of a typical body shop, and the company's goal is to operate a 100% emission-free auto body business.

Creative Paper Wales[12]

Creative Paper Wales (Wales, United Kingdom) makes only recycled paper products. All manufacturing processes are environmentally friendly and minimize waste. The company supports Fair Trade. Creative Paper Wales is home to the ever popular Sheep Poo Paper and Reindeer Poo Paper, made from sheep and reindeer dung, respectively. The company offers to make paper from anything you desire, except live trees.

CREDO Mobile[13]

CREDO Mobile (San Francisco, California) was created in 1985 to help make the world a better place. Every time customers use their wireless, credit card, or long-distance services, the company donates a portion of the charges to progressive nonprofit organizations working for peace, human rights, economic justice, education, and the environment. The company offsets its carbon emissions, and innovative mobile activism allows subscribers to stay on top of fast-moving and progressive issues and take action right from their phones.

Earth Class Mail[14]

Earth Class Mail (Seattle, Washington) offers online post office boxes and mail services. Customers view scanned images of mail received and, for each piece, they make a decision to open and scan the contents, recycle, archive, or forward the mail to them via surface mail. The company's Web site states that the average person recycles 20% of their mail, whereas Earth Class Mail customers recycle more than 90% of their mail.

Earth Tones[15]

Earth Tones (Denver, Colorado) bills itself as "The Environmental Internet & Phone Company." The company offers Internet access and long-distance and wireless phone services. Earth Tones is a for-profit company created in 1993 by a coalition of nonprofit environmental organizations. The company donates 100% of profits to environmental organizations, including Environment America, National Environmental Law Center, the Green Life, Campaign to Save the Environment, Toxics Action Center, ecopledge.com, Free the Planet!, and Recycling Action Campaign. Earth Tones offers online billing or (recycled) paper billing and phone recycling for customers. In addition, the Web site has resources available to everyone, including Green Alerts and a marketplace.

ECO Car Wash[16]

ECO Car Wash (Portland, Oregon) is a multilocation car wash that recycles 100% of the water used in washing. The car wash's computer-controlled water management system uses 25 to 40 gallons of freshwater per vehicle wash, far less than hand washing at home. Additionally, ECO Car Wash uses water-soluble, bio-based, and biodegradable cleaning products. Furthermore, the company uses wind energy in all facilities. To support the community, ECO Car Wash makes contributions to several charitable organizations, including Providence Hospital, Shriners Hospital, the Grotto, and Children's Charity Ball.

Eco-Libris[17]

Eco-Libris (Newark, Deleware) is a carbon offset program. Book lovers and reading aficionados everywhere can buy an "offset" for every book they read. At Eco-Libris, the idea is simple: People can plant 1.3 trees for every book they read. Eco-Libris' planting partners plant trees in Nicaragua, Belize, Guatemala, Honduras, Panama (all in Central America) and Malawi (Africa).

EDUN[18]

EDUN (Dublin, Ireland) is a socially conscious clothing company launched to create sustainable employment in developing countries. EDUN has established the Conservation Cotton Initiative (CCI) to improve the livelihoods of communities in Africa by promoting cotton grown organically or through methods that are part of a transition from conventional to organic production. CCI also works to incorporate sustainable conservation agricultural practices and the protection of wildlife. In addition to the EDUN retail collection of items made with organic cotton, edun LIVE[19] is a business-to-business solution for anyone who wants ethically produced blank T-shirts. Edun LIVE seeks to provide sustainable employment in Sub-Saharan Africa through high-volume sales of blank T-shirts. As part of edun LIVE, the company has created edun LIVE on campus,[20] a partnership with Miami University of Ohio, to sell blank T-shirts to campus organizations with the goal to eventually expand to additional campuses. EDUN and edun LIVE products are currently produced in India, Peru, Tunisia, Kenya, Lesotho, Mauritius, and Madagascar. The company works with Verite for third-party monitoring and reporting of socially responsible business practices.

Fair Trade Sports[21]

Fair Trade Sports (Bainbridge Island, Washington) is a sports ball and equipment distributor and manufacturer. The company ensures all its hand-stitched balls are made by adults who are paid fair wages and who are provided healthy working environments. Additionally, since the sports ball business can be seasonal, the company offers microcredit loans to workers. The inner air bladders of the balls are made with FSC-certified latex from rubber plantations and then sent to Pakistan for assembly into sports balls. In the first ever Fair Trade deal with a plantation, Fair Trade Sports sources rubber from the Frocester Plantation in Sri Lanka and from the New Ambadi Rubber Estate. Following the deal with Fair Trade Sports, the Frocester Plantation then created the Fair Trade Welfare Society for the plantation's rubber tappers and employees. Early funds generated from the Society led to the installation of a pump and piping system for nearby plantation households to access well water and to the restoration of a restroom facility on the plantation. All after-tax profits of Fair Trade Sports are donated to children's charities to help at-risk children around the world.

FIO360[22]

FIO360 (Atlanta, Georgia) is the nation's first eco-early care and learning boutique. The building is the first child care center to be LEED-certified and has floors that emit radiant heat and are made from virgin rubber plants, paint that is zero-VOC (volatile organic compounds), and solar tubes for lighting. The center uses organic furnishings, such as imported organic rugs, organic wooden toys, no PVC plastic products, and organic mattresses free of formaldehyde and other chemicals. Children are served organic and hormone-free meals using local fresh ingredients created by the center's chef. The center also uses nontoxic personal care products on children and environmentally friendly cleaning products throughout the building. The curriculum is holistic, promotes multicultural awareness and learning, and, of course, environmental education.

Free Range Studios[23]

Free Range Studios (Washington, DC) is a full-service creative agency delivering progressive socially minded messages for clients. You may be familiar with some of Free Range Studios's flash movies (e.g., Sam Suds, The Meatrix, Friends With Low Wages, Grocery Store Wars, Say No to Blood Diamonds), written reports (prepared for Amnesty International, Green Mountain Coffee Roasters, and the ACLU), or the company's work with socially conscious individuals, nonprofits, and businesses. In addition to Free Range Studio's socially conscious creative work, the company also seeks to reduce its environmental impact and give back to communities through the use of triple bottom line accounting, 100% wind power, eco-printing, and other initiatives.

Frog's Leap Winery[24]

Frog's Leap Winery (Rutherford, California) is committed to sustainable farming and traditional farming techniques, including dry farming, which requires tilling every 10 days to hold moisture and which eliminates the need for irrigation. All wines are made from organically grown grapes. The winery has been 100% solar-powered since 2005, and the Hospitality Center and administrative offices are in a LEED-certified building.

Gaia Napa Valley Hotel and Spa[25]

Gaia Napa Valley Hotel and Spa (American Canyon, California) is the world's first Gold LEED–certified hotel. To achieve this, all wood used in the construction was FSC-certified, paints are low VOC, and carpets contain postconsumer recycled material. In addition, restroom construction used recycled tiles and granite, and low flush toilets and showerheads were installed. The hotel's koi pond uses filtered recycled water, and the facility installed Solatube lighting, solar panels, and a reflective roof coating. The hotel is furnished with natural, organic, and recycled materials, has all-natural and organic landscaping, and uses green cleaning products. To reduce waste, bulk soap, lotion, and shampoo dispensers are used in guest rooms and only recycled paper is used. There are recycling bins throughout the property, and educational kiosks inform guests of the environmental attributes of the property.

Galactic Pizza[26]

Galactic Pizza (Minneapolis, Minnesota) makes excellent pizza from local and organic ingredients. The company emphasizes environmental and social responsibility in its operations. The company engages in many sustainability initiatives. For example, when possible, electric vehicles are used for deliveries, the restaurant uses 100% renewable wind energy, organic items are on the menu, purchase of the Second Harvest Heartland pizza generates a $1 donation to this hunger relief organization, packaging is either made from recycled materials or is biodegradable, hemp products are on the menu, the menus are printed on hemp paper, produce comes from farms in Minnesota or Wisconsin when possible, the company recycles and composts, and 5% of pretax profits are donated to charity.

Great Elephant Poo Poo Paper Company Ltd.[27]

The Great Elephant Poo Poo Paper Company Ltd. (Toronto, Ontario) recycles the waste of African and Asian elephants from elephant conservation parks and turns it into over 150 unique (and odorless) paper products. The paper products are handcrafted by artisans. A portion of profits is donated to elephant welfare and conservation programs.

Great Lakes Brewing Company[28]

Great Lakes Brewing Company (Cleveland, Ohio) is a microbrewery focused on the triple bottom line. The company recycles waste, uses recycled products, and has invested in energy efficiency. To pursue sustainability even further, Great Lakes Brewing Company has incorporated zero-waste initiatives into its day-to-day operations. The ultimate goal is to mimic nature, where 100% of resources are used in closed-loop ecosystems. This is accomplished in several ways. Certain bread and pretzels found on the menu are made using grains from the brewing process.

Brewery grains are also used as a substrate for growing organic shitake and oyster mushrooms. And the company also composts waste to create fertilizer to grow herbs and vegetables for menu items. In addition, the beer delivery truck, the Fatty Wagon, runs on 100% pure vegetable oil.

Green Microgym[29]

The Green Microgym (Portland, Oregon) is one of the few fitness facilities in the world operating partially on solar and human power. While the facility is fully equipped with all the standard equipment found in any gym, the equipment has been retrofitted to capture, store, and reuse energy produced from the use of elliptical trainers and stationary bikes. The company has a goal of net-zero energy usage. The "Burn & Earn" program pays members $1 for every hour spent generating (or saving) electricity. The Green Microgym uses recycled rubber, marmoleum, and eco-friendly cork flooring, ENERGY STAR ceiling fans, LCD televisions, compact fluorescent bulbs, energy-efficient treadmills, dual flush toilets, green cleaning supplies, and paper products made with recycled content.

Greenforce[30]

Greenforce (San Francisco, California) offers residential and commercial cleaning services using environmentally friendly cleaning products and methods. The company uses natural nontoxic biodegradable supplies and HEPA microfiltered vacuums. Greenforce thoroughly researches cleaning products to find those that perform as well as conventional products, and all staff are trained in green cleaning methods. On its Web site, Greenforce lists the products used and recommended by the company. In addition to eco-friendly cleaning, Greenforce offsets emissions created from travel to its cleaning sites (carbon neutral cleaning).

Greyston Bakery[31]

Greyston Bakery (Yonkers, New York) is an example of social entrepreneurship at its finest. The for-profit bakery was started to provide employment opportunities and economic renewal for this inner-city community. All profits from Greyston Bakery go to support the

Greyston Foundation, which offers affordable child care for the community, affordable housing for homeless and low-income families, and affordable health care for persons with HIV. The bakery's facility was selected as a Top Ten Green Project in 2004 for its use of natural light, rooftop gardens, efficient machinery, and the use of outdoor air to cool baked goods. The bakery produces many traditional baked goods but is well known as the exclusive supplier of brownies for Ben & Jerry's ice cream products.

Habana Outpost[32]

Habana Outpost (Brooklyn, New York) is a one-of-a-kind restaurant experience that begins with the outdoor food truck, a restored U.S. postal service truck. Habana Outpost is solar-powered; has both indoor and outdoor seating; uses compostable biodegradable plates, cups, and utensils; has tables made from recycled materials; operates a rainwater collection system to water plants and flush toilets; runs a human-powered bicycle-propelled juice blender; and composts and recycles waste.

In addition to these restaurant features, Habana Outpost serves as a community gathering place offering weekly movie nights and a host of other activities. For example, the Kid's Corner offers ecological activities and an "alternative heroes" coloring book (about real-life heroes!). The restaurant hosts a weekend market of local vendors and weekly fashion shows for local designers. The restaurant also hosts an annual Earth Day Expo of informative and interactive displays on sustainability and has a gallery display featuring local artists' works.

Habana Outpost is one of three Habana restaurants in New York City. The company operates Habana Works, Inc., a nonprofit offering free sustainability-related workshops through various programs such as Habana Labs and Urban Studio Brooklyn. Habana Labs is dedicated to researching, developing, applying, and teaching the best technology related to ecology and sustainable energy. The most recent Habana Labs project is the Offgrid Outlet, a motorized, sun-following solar panel. Another program of Habana Works is the Urban Studio Brooklyn, an architectural design and build program that recently launched the Fishmobile, a human-powered mobile fishing clinic and wetlab.

Higher Grounds Trading Company[33]

Higher Grounds Trading Company (Traverse City, Michigan) sells organic and Fair Trade coffee. But the company's commitment to sustainability goes beyond the products it sells. The company has a strong environmental emphasis in supporting sustainable agriculture, recycling, composting, and purchasing postconsumer recycled paper for office supplies.

The company has an even stronger social emphasis through its business operations. The Trade for a Change fund-raising program allows nonprofit organizations to sell Higher Grounds's organic and Fair Trade blends and thus increases sales for the coffee farmers. Sales of Coffees for Change blends generate donations for organic agriculture, education about economic justice, protection of bird habitat and indigenous rights, and the construction of potable water systems. Sales of Water Carrier's Blend generate a $5 donation through the Water for All campaign for the construction of sustainable water systems in coffee-growing countries.

Through the Oromia Photo Project, Oromia Coffee Farmers Grower Union farmers' activities are documented. Each week, new photos are added to the Web site so that you can learn more about how the coffee is produced. For each pound of the Ethiopian Oromia coffee sold, Higher Grounds will add an additional $1 tip to go back to the farmers.

Higher Grounds's Fair Trade Tours invites you to join them on a trip to partner farms and Fair Trade collaborators. You can choose from trips to Africa, Central America, or South America, and $100 per participant is donated to a local project.

Hopworks Urban Brewery[34]

Hopworks Urban Brewery (Portland, Oregon) is a brewpub offering organic beer and restaurant menu items made from local ingredients. Hopworks Urban Brewery refers to itself as an eco-brewpub and touts everything from composting to rain barrels to being powered by 100% renewable energy. The brew kettle uses biodiesel, the pizza oven heat is captured to heat the brewing water, the delivery truck uses biodiesel, and hot water from the wort heat exchanger is recovered for subsequent brew. There were many recycled and recovered materials used in the remodeling process, low and zero-VOC finishes were used, a rain barrel collection system was installed, and native landscaping is being used. The brewery also installed water and energy efficient equipment, designed for the use of natural lighting, and offers bicycle parking and a bike repair stand. The company's waste recycling programs strive for zero waste and recycles food waste for animal feed and composting.

Hotlips Pizza[35]

Hotlips Pizza (Portland, Oregon) is a family-owned four-restaurant business. Hotlips Pizza uses as many locally grown ingredients as possible, including wheat, vegetables, cheese, and meat. The company tracks food miles, uses LED lighting, delivers pizza by bicycle or electric car, captures the heat from pizza ovens to heat the water, composts waste, and is exploring alternative fuel use to heat the pizza ovens.

Immaculate Baking Company[36]

Immaculate Baking Company (Hendersonville, North Carolina) bakes delicious gourmet all-natural and organic baked cookies and organic ready-to-bake cookie dough. The company philosophy is "Bake well, be creative, have fun and give back." Immaculate Baking Company works hard to maximize its social impact by baking "Cookies With a Cause." The company created the Folk Artist's Foundation to provide support and exposure for folk artists. Folk art also adorns all cookie packaging. In addition, the company created Soul Food Fund "artreach" programs to reach kids of all ages to help them creatively express themselves. As an aside, the company holds the distinction of baking the World's Biggest Cookie in 2003—102 feet wide and over 40,000 pounds.

Indigenous Designs[37]

Indigenous Designs (Santa Rosa, California) sells organic Fair Trade fashions created by their own artisan network across South America. All items are handmade by artisans using traditional techniques, natural colors, natural dyes, and low-impact dyes. Indigenous Designs also partners with nongovernmental organizations and others to help provide training, educational materials, and equipment to the artisans.

In addition to organic Fair Trade fashions, Indigenous Designs purchases local green power to offset carbon emissions from its business activities, encourages employees to bike to work, and claims that about 20% of employees own and drive hybrid or biodiesel cars.

IceStone[38]

IceStone (Brooklyn, New York) manufactures surfaces made from recycled glass and concrete. By recycling glass and concrete, IceStone saves hundreds of tons of glass from landfills each year. The products are cradle to cradle certified and are manufactured in a day-lit factory. The factory has a cool, low-emissions manufacturing process. IceStone is working to become carbon-neutral, purchases renewable energy credits, and strives to reduce energy usage. The company is working toward water reduction goals, and over 80% of the company's waste is recycled, recovered, or composted. IceStone is implementing a greywater recycling system. All petroleum-based machine lubricants have been replaced with soy-based lubricants. Additionally, IceStone conducts environmental education programs for employees.

IceStone's mission also provides living wages, health benefits, education programs, and life skill training to employees, including free English as a Second Language classes, all of which are tracked in the social audit with third-party verification. IceStone's donation program provides free or discounted material to projects that share similar social and environmental goals, with Habitat for Humanity receiving annual donations. The company also partners with community, nonprofit, academic, industrial assistance, and local social services groups to promote green-collar job creation, sustainable business practices, and the development of the green building industry.

Within the supply chain, IceStone encourages suppliers to improve sustainability standards. IceStone's glass and mother-of-pearl are recycled from post-industrial and post-consumer sources. IceStone advocates for stronger glass recycling programs in New York in order to create an infrastructure that allows the commercial reuse of regional waste glass. The company buys cement regionally and advocates for the greening of the cement industry. IceStone continuously conducts product research to seek the most eco-friendly and local materials possible.

Izzy's Ice Cream Café[39]

Izzy's Ice Cream Café (St. Paul, Minnesota) makes homemade ice cream using local ingredients, when possible, such as local maple syrup and dairy and cream from local and family-owned farms. Since making and freezing ice cream is an energy-intensive process, the ice cream parlor runs entirely on solar power. The shop is organizing to put more solar panels on its roof in order to supply solar power to the neighborhood. The company also delivers ice cream in thermo-insulated bags instead of refrigerated trucks.

Keen Footwear[40]

Keen Footwear (Portland, Oregon) began in 2003 with the Hybrid: part shoe, part sandal; a cross between an athletic shoe and a sandal. The company now has a line of shoes, Ventura, that are 100% vegan and created through environmentally friendly manufacturing processes. The Transport bag collection is made from recycled aluminum and rubber reclaimed from the shoe factory floors. Even the packaging is environmentally friendly with shoe boxes made of 100% recycled materials, soy-based inks, water-based glues, and biodegradable materials. The shoe boxes are smaller than standard shoe boxes, resulting in less materials, labor, and waste.

Keen Footwear uses third-party independent monitoring of its operations, is seeking Fair Labor Association accreditation, and is currently preparing its first Accountability Report, following the Global Reporting Initiative guidelines. The Keen Foundation supports environmental and social causes.

Little Rock Green Garage[41]

Little Rock Green Garage (Little Rock, Arkansas) is attempting to embrace environmental sustainability through all aspects of its operations and seeks to become one of the country's first green auto repair facilities. The garage recycles waste, buys in bulk, uses refillable containers, and specializes in the repair of fuel-efficient vehicles.

LJ Urban[42]

LJ Urban (Sacramento, California) is a real estate development company that has set out to be a catalyst of social change. One of the company's interesting projects involves building an eco-urban community, appropriately named The Good Project. The Good Project consists of LEED-certified homes with ENERGY STAR appliances, solar panels, air intake air-conditioning, tankless water heaters, dual flush toilets, low-flow plumbing fixtures, reflective roofing, recycled countertops and insulation, compact fluorescent lights and occupancy sensors, and more eco-friendly features. The Good Project I is complete, and the company is now creating the Good Project II, which will also feature a community garden in the design. One of the most unique parts of the Good Project I was the Do-Some-Good-Now Commitment. For every eco-urban home sold, LJ Urban trained a local mason in West Africa to build sustainable homes. LJ Urban's Good Projects were inspired by the simplicity of TOMS Shoes's model of giving away a pair of shoes to children in need for every pair that was purchased.

Llamadas Pedaleadas (Pedaled Phone Calls)[43]

Llamadas Pedaleadas (Managua, Nicaragua), or Pedaled Phone Calls, is a bicycle-pedaled mobile cart with public telephones on board. Recycling parts found in a junkyard, the company created a battery that can be recharged by pedal power. Electricity is generated as the person is traveling to his destination. If the battery runs low at the destination, he can drop the kickstand and start cycling in place. The mobile cart can be moved to any location, such as a park or festival, to provide public telephone service for consumers. The company's goal is to create a ready-made business for local entrepreneurs and to increase access to affordable telephony for base of the pyramid customers.

Massanelli's Cleaners[44]

Massanelli's Cleaners (Jonesboro, Arkansas) offers dry-cleaning and fire-water recovery and restoration services. Massanelli's Cleaners utilizes a completely environmentally friendly nontoxic, odorless cleaning process that has been thoroughly tested by the Environmental Protection Agency and causes neither short nor long-term health risks. Cleaning agents are 100% biodegradable and earth-friendly, and the perchloroethylene-free (perc-free) cleaning process is gentle not only on your clothing and textiles but also on the environment.

In an effort to further reduce the carbon footprint of Massanelli's Cleaners, the company has joined the CarbonFree Small Business Program. The company has been recognized for environmental stewardship and was an official sponsor of the Green Jobs Now fair held at the University of Arkansas at Little Rock. Massanelli's Cleaners supports numerous charitable organizations and has a strong philanthropy program.

Natural Fusion Hair Studio[45]

Natural Fusion Hair Studio (Frederick, Maryland) is an environmentally friendly hair salon. The salon seeks to reduce energy and water usage throughout its operations, recycles, uses nontoxic environmentally friendly cleaners, refills bottles, uses only natural and organic hair and beauty products, and purchases from beauty supply companies with sustainable practices. In addition, the salon gives back to the community and local charities. Located in a historic house, when they remodeled they preserved the original wood floors and added linoleum floors where new flooring was needed. The cutting stations are 1920s vanities, and the salon has utilized antiques whenever possible.

Peace Cereal[46]

Golden Temple's Peace Cereal (Eugene, Oregon) is a line of organic cereals devoted to personal health and a peaceful planet. Ten percent of the proceeds from Peace Cereal sponsor the annual International Peace Prayer Day gathering. The company gives awards to peace activists and grants to nonprofit organizations working for peace. In addition, Peace Cereal founded the Socially Responsible Business Awards.

Pinehurst Inn[47]

Pinehurst Inn Bed & Breakfast (Bayfield, Wisconsin) is a historic inn, built in 1885. The Pinehurst Inn uses solar hot water heaters, green cleaning products, and organic linens and towels. Pinehurst Inn composts food and garden waste, recycles, avoids chemical treatments on lawn and gardens, serves locally grown organic food and organic coffees and teas, and has converted their vehicle (the Grease Car) to run on recycled grease. In 2003, the owners added the Garden House, a green building that is energy-efficient and that used sustainable materials in construction. The Pinehurst Inn also purchases carbon offsets for the business as well as offsets for 50% of customers' travel to the inn.

Pizza Fusion[48]

Pizza Fusion (Fort Lauderdale, Florida) is a pizza chain with a wide variety of organic, vegan, gluten-free, and lactose-free menu items. Seventy-five percent of the menu is organic; the company only uses all-natural free-range chicken and organic beef, and it serves organic drinks.

Each month, Pizza Fusion hosts fun lessons on sustainability through "Organics 101" for kids. The company delivers pizzas in company-owned hybrid vehicles, uses compostable food containers, and offsets 100% of power consumption through renewable energy certificates. Each franchise restaurant is LEED certified. Pizza Fusion also encourages customers to return their pizza boxes for recycling, and the Web site offers tips for sustainable living alongside a carbon footprint calculator.

sweetriot[49]

Trendy chocolatier sweetriot (New York, New York) makes all-natural chocolate treats (called "peaces") and works to create a more just and celebrated multicultural world. sweetriot gets its all-natural cacao from countries of origin in Latin America and abides by ethical and FairTrade sourcing. The finished dark chocolate–covered cacao goodies are packaged in recycled and reusable tins featuring the work of emerging artists. If you do not have local recycling facilities, the company encourages you to return your tin to them for recycling. sweetriot offsets all employee travel and office emissions and offers customers the option to offset carbon dioxide emissions for shipping their order. The company promotes fair human resources practices and work–life balance, and it also supports nonprofits that share similar values and ideals.

SunNight Solar[50]

SunNight Solar (Houston, Texas) is a company focused on the triple bottom line that makes solar-powered flashlights. The lights are rugged and durable and suited for harsh conditions in which no light is available. The lights use a low-environmental impact battery and can be used for either task lighting or room lighting. The solar-powered lights offer an alternative to kerosene, wood, and other forms of lighting used in developing countries.

SunNight Solar is home to the extremely popular BoGo Light program. For each flashlight purchased, the company donates one flashlight to a nonprofit for distribution in a developing country and gives them $1 per flashlight to offset importation and distribution costs. The company sponsors several campaigns that maximize its social impact. Lights for Good is a fund-raising partnership with nonprofit organizations. WarLights allows you to purchase a flashlight for distribution to American troops in Iraq and Afghanistan. Three new giving programs are being developed: Save Our Sisters (which will donate lights to women's groups and collectives in developing countries), Village Lights, and Need It/Take It.

Thanksgiving Coffee Company[51]

Thanksgiving Coffee Company (Fort Bragg, California) roasts Fair Trade, organic, and kosher blends of coffee. The company purchases coffee beans directly from small family farms and cooperatives in Guatemala, Ethiopia, Rwanda, Uganda, and Nicaragua. The company partners with nonprofits to support sustainable farming practices and environmental causes. The company recycles, composts, uses biodiesel in delivery trucks, and uses recycled paper. In 2002, the company purchased its first carbon offsets and became the first carbon neutral coffee company.

TOMS Shoes[52]

TOMS Shoes (Santa Monica, California) was founded with the singular mission of improving the lives of children by providing shoes to those in need. Shoes are produced in Argentina and China following fair labor practices while creating minimal environmental impact. Factories are monitored by TOMS and third-party independent auditors. TOMS Shoes are sold online and in retail locations around the world with the promise that for each pair purchased, TOMS will give one pair to a child in need in Argentina, South Africa, and other locations around the world. To date, TOMS has donated over 60,000 pairs of shoes during Shoe Drops around the world. Through its nonprofit, Friends of TOMS, the public is invited to participate in Shoe Drops. The documentary *For Tomorrow: The TOMS Shoe Story* follows the early days of the company and its initial Shoe Drops.

Tropical Salvage[53]

Tropical Salvage (Portland, Oregon) is a tropical wood furniture company that never cuts down a single tree to make a product. Items are made from reclaimed wood and trees from rivers and lakes; flood, landslide, and volcanic debris; and construction sites. The wood and trees are then transported to one of two facilities in Indonesia where artisans build, carve, and finish the wood to create beautiful furniture and decorative items. Items are then shipped to North America for retail sale. Tropical Salvage is collaborating with the nonprofit Institute for Culture and Ecology to create the Jepara Forest Conservancy, a public forest park and environmental education facility.

VerTerra[54]

VerTerra (New York, New York) is a manufacturer of disposable dinnerware. Plates, bowls, and cups are made from 100% renewable and compostable plant matter and water. The products are created by collecting fallen leaves from plantations, taken to the factory, sprayed with high pressure water, steamed, and UV sterilized. In the manufacturing process, the company recaptures over 80% of the water used. No chemicals, lacquers, glues, bonding agents, or toxins are ever used. The entire process uses only a fraction of the typical energy used for recycling. The disposable dinnerware products are durable, naturally biodegrade in 2 months, and can be used in the microwave, oven, and refrigerator. Items are made in South Asia by VerTerra's own employees where employees receive fair wages in safe working conditions and are provided access to health care.

White Bear Racquet and Swim Club[55]

White Bear Racquet and Swim Club (White Bear Lake, Minnesota) has fully embraced sustainability. The sustainability section of the club's Web site outlines the many initiatives the company has undertaken in the quest for a more environmentally friendly facility. While too numerous to list, here is a small sampling of what the company has accomplished.

White Bear Racquet and Swim Club has replaced incandescent lights; increased the use of natural lighting; replaced chlorine with a salt water system for the pool; replaced a five–tennis court bubble with a permanent, super insulated tennis building featuring in-court radiant heat, installed cooling, and heating powered by ground source heat pumps (the old courts required over $44,000 in heating costs; the new courts require less than $300 in heating costs); and installed a super efficient lighting system. In addition, White Bear Racquet and Swim Club installed water-saving showerheads, restored outside land to its natural state (eliminating the need for watering, mowing, and fertilizing), reduced waste, began using local and organic foods, began using natural green cleaning products, and incorporated office furniture that is made from renewable or recycled materials and can all be recycled.

White Dog Café[56]

The White Dog Café (Philadelphia, Pennsylvania) is a restaurant that supports sustainable agriculture by purchasing seasonal, local, organic ingredients from local farmers whenever possible. In addition to supporting sustainable agriculture, the White Dog Café partners with "sister" restaurants in the area that are minority-owned. This project encourages customers to visit neighborhoods they otherwise might not visit and to support minority-owned businesses and cultural institutions. The sister restaurant project also has an international dimension to foster awareness, communication, and economic justice worldwide. The international program offers educational tours to the countries of international sister restaurants, a chef exchange program, hosts international visitors, and promotes Fair Trade.

White Dog Café has a mentoring program with a local high school's restaurant, hotel, and tourism program, organizes community tours through different Philadelphia neighborhoods, hosts annual multicultural events, participates in Take a Senior to Lunch Day, and hosts speakers each month on various social and policy issues. White Dog Café donates an amazing 20% of pretax profits to nonprofits and the café has also created its own nonprofit, White Dog Community Enterprises.

Zambezi Organic Forest Honey[57]

Zambezi Organic Forest Honey (Oxford, Ohio) was founded by former Peace Corps volunteers who spent time in Zambia, Africa. Zambezi Organic Forest Honey helps local Zambian beekeepers access new markets for the organic honey that the Lunda people have been farming as a way of life for over 500 years.

Zambian beekeepers who register with the company cooperative gain access to free training on sustainable beekeeping, agriculture, and forestry practices; free education for literacy, mathematics, and small-business skills; free beekeeping supplies; and farmers are under no obligation to sell solely to the company, fostering further economic growth of the region. The company pays, on average, 40% above market prices for the organic honey, and the company collective currently has 5,000 registered beekeepers. In addition, Zambezi Honey donates a portion of profits back to Zambia for projects in malaria prevention, HIV/AIDS education, school scholarships, and rural-income generation grants.

APPENDIX

Resources for the Sustainable Business

AA1000 Framework
AccountAbility
250-252 Goswell Road
London
EC1V 7EB
United Kingdom
Tel: +4420 7549 0400
Fax: +4420 7253 74400
250 24th Street NW, Suite 300
Washington, DC 20037
USA
Tel: (202) 835-1692
Fax: (202) 835-1693
E-mail: secretariat@accountability21.net
Web: http://www.accountability21.net

AA1000 Stakeholder Engagement Standard
AccountAbility
250-252 Goswell Road
London
EC1V 7EB
United Kingdom
Tel: +4420 7549 0400
Fax: +4420 7253 74400

250 24th Street NW, Suite 300
Washington, DC 20037
USA
Tel: (202) 835-1692
Fax: (202) 835-1693
E-mail: secretariat@accountability21.net
Web: http://www.accountability21.net/uploadedFiles/publications/
SES%20Exposure%20Draft%20-%20FullPDF.pdf

AA1000 Assurance Standard
AccountAbility
250-252 Goswell Road
London
EC1V 7EB
United Kingdom
Tel: +4420 7549 0400
Fax: +4420 7253 74400
250 24th Street NW, Suite 300
Washington, DC 20037
USA
Tel: (202) 835-1692
Fax: (202) 835-1693
E-mail: secretariat@accountability21.net
Web: http://www.accountability21.net/uploadedFiles/publications/
AA1000AS%202008.pdf

AccountAbility
250-252 Goswell Road
London
EC1V 7EB
United Kingdom
Tel: +4420 7549 0400
Fax: +4420 7253 74400
250 24th Street NW, Suite 300
Washington, DC 20037
USA
Tel: (202) 835-1692
Fax: (202) 835-1693

E-mail: secretariat@accountability21.net
Web: http://www.accountability21.net

Acre Resources Ltd.
131-151 Great Titchfield Street
London
W1W 5BB
United Kingdom
Tel: United Kingdom: +0845 257 8030; International: +44 20 3170 8030
Fax: +44 20 3008 7759
E-mail: mail@acre-resources.co.uk
Web: http://www.acre-resources.co.uk

Apollo Alliance
330 Townsend Street, Suite 205
San Francisco, CA 94107
USA
Tel: (415) 371-1700
Fax: (415) 371-1707
E-mail: comments@apolloalliance.org
Web: http://apolloalliance.org

Apparel Industry Partnership
American Apparel & Footwear Association
1601 N Kent St FL 12
Arlington, VA 22209
USA
Tel: (703) 524-1864
E-mail: jmcneal@apparelandfootwear.org
Web: http://www.apparelandfootwear.org

Applied Sustainability Center
University of Arkansas at Fayetteville
Sam M. Walton College of Business, Building 475
1 University of Arkansas
Fayetteville, AR 72701
USA

Tel: (479) 575-4594
Web: http://asc.uark.edu

AskNature.org
Web: http://www.asknature.org

Aspen Institute
Business & Society Program
One Dupont Circle NW, Suite 700
Washington, DC 20036-1133
USA
Tel: (202) 736-5800
Fax: (202) 467-0790
E-mail: info@aspenbsp.org
Web: http://www.aspeninstitute.org

Aspen Principles, The
Business & Society Program
One Dupont Circle NW, Suite 700
Washington, DC 20036-1133
USA
Tel: (202) 736-5800
Fax: (202) 467-0790
E-mail: info@aspenbsp.org
Web: http://www.aspeninstitute.org/atf/cf/%7BDEB6F227-659B-4EC8
   -8F84-8DF23CA704F5%7D/FinalPrinciples.pdf

Association of British Insurers
51 Gresham Street
London EC2V 7HQ
United Kingdom
Tel: +44 20 7600 3333
Fax: +44 20 7696 8999
E-mail: info@abi.org.uk
Web: http://www.abi.org.uk

Australian Computer Society
Level 3, 160 Clarence Street
Sydney NSW 2000
Australia

Tel: +61 2 9299 3666
Fax: +61 2 9299 3997
E-mail: info@acs.org.au
Web: http://www.acs.org.au

B Corporation
B Lab
8 Walnut Avenue
Berwyn, PA 19312
USA
Tel: (610) 296-8283
Fax: (610) 296-8289
E-mail: thelab@bcorporation.net
Web: http://www.bcorporation.net

Balanced Scorecard Institute
975 Walnut Street, Suite 360
Cary, NC 27511
USA
Tel: (919) 460-8180
Fax: (919) 460-0867
Web: http://www.balancedscorecard.org

Base of the Pyramid Protocol 2.0
Center for Sustainable Global Enterprise
Johnson Graduate School of Management
Cornell University
142 Sage Hall
Ithaca, NY 14853
USA
Tel: (607) 255-0276
Web: http://www.bop-protocol.org/docs/BoPProtocol2ndEdition2008
   .pdf

Bay Area Green Business Program
Association of Bay Area Governments
101 Eighth Street
Oakland, CA 94607
USA

Tel: (510) 464-7900
Web: http://www.greenbiz.ca.gov

Biomimicry Guild
PO Box 575
Helena, MT 59624
USA
Tel: (406) 495-1858
E-mail: habitat@biomimicryguild.com
Web: http://www.biomimicryguild.com

Biomimicry Institution
PO Box 9216
Missoula, MT 59807
USA
Tel: (406) 728-4134
Web: http://www.biomimicryinstitute.org

Business Alliance for Local Living Economies (BALLE)
1002B O'Reilly Avenue
San Francisco, CA 94129
USA
Tel: (415) 255-1108
E-mail: info@livingeconomies.org
Web: http://www.livingeconomies.org

Business Council for Peace (Bpeace)
5 E. 22nd Street, Suite 9J
New York, NY 10010
USA
Tel: (212) 696-9696
E-mail: websiteinquiry@bpeace.org
Web: http://www.bpeace.org

Business Ethics Magazine
55 West 39th Street, Suite 800
New York, NY 10018
USA
Tel: (212) 537-9381
Fax: (212) 202-3561

E-mail: info@business-ethics.com
Web: http://www.business-ethics.com

Business for Social Responsibility
111 Sutter Street, 12th Floor
San Francisco, CA 94104
USA
Tel: (415) 984-3200
Fax: (415) 984-3201
E-mail: web@bsr.org
Web: http://www.bsr.org

Caux Round Table Self-Assessment and Improvement Process
Caux Round Table Principles
6 West Fifth Street, #300M
Saint Paul, MN 55102
USA
Tel: (651) 223-2852
Fax: (612) 573-6565
E-mail: steve@cauxroundtable.net
Web: http://www.cauxroundtable.org

Center for Business as an Agent of World Benefit
Case Western Reserve University
208 Peter B. Lewis Building
11119 Bellflower Road
Cleveland, OH 44106-7235
USA
Tel: (216) 368-2160
E-mail: bawb@case.edu
Web: http://worldbenefit.case.edu

Center for Companies That Care
500 N. Dearborn Street, 2nd Floor
Chicago, IL 60654
USA
Tel: (312) 661-1010
E-mail: info@companies-that-care.org
Web: http://www.companies-that-care.org

Center for Corporate Citizenship
Boston College Center for Corporate Citizenship
Carroll School of Management
55 Lee Road
Chestnut Hill, MA 02467-3942
USA
Tel: (617) 552-4545
Fax: (617) 552-8499
E-mail: ccc@bc.edu
Web: http://www.bcccc.net

Center for Responsible Business (CRB)
University of California, Berkeley
Haas School of Business
545 Student Services, Building 1900
Berkeley, CA 94720-1900
USA
Tel: (510) 643-7668
E-mail: respbus@haas.berkeley.edu
Web: http://www.haas.berkeley.edu/responsiblebusiness

Center for Sustainable Business Practices
Beth Hjelm, Interim Managing Director
Lundquist College of Business
University of Oregon
1208 University of Oregon, Gilbert Hall
Eugene, OR 97403-1208
USA
Tel: (541) 346-1493
E-mail: bhjelm@uoregon.edu
Web: http://lcb.uoregon.edu/csbp

Center for Sustainable Enterprise
George Nassos, Director
Illinois Institute of Technology
Stuart School of Business
565 West Adams Street
Chicago, IL 60661
USA

Tel: (312) 906-6543
E-mail: gnassos@stuart.iit.edu
Web: http://www.stuart.iit.edu/cse

Center for Sustainable Global Enterprise
Johnson Graduate School of Management
142 Sage Hall
Cornell University
Ithaca, NY 14853
USA
Tel: (607) 255-0276
E-mail: csge@cornell.edu
Web: http://www.johnson.cornell.edu/sge

Center for the Development of Social Finance
PMB 168
6327 SW Capitol Highway, Suite C
Portland, OR 97239
USA
Tel: (503) 333-2275
E-mail: cdsfinfo@cdsofi.org
Web: http://www.cdsofi.org

CEOs Without Borders
35 Claremont Avenue 3s
New York, NY 10027
USA
E-mail: info@ceoswb.org
Web: http://www.ceoswb.org

Certified B Corporation
8 Walnut Avenue
Berwyn, PA 19312
USA
Tel: (610) 296-8283
Fax: (610) 296-8289
E-mail: thelab@bcorporation.net
Web: http://www.bcorporation.net

Chicago Climate Exchange (CCX)
190 South LaSalle Street, Suite 1100
Chicago, IL 60603
USA
Tel: (312) 554-3350
Fax: (312) 554-3373
E-mail: info@chicagoclimatex.com
Web: http://www.chicagoclimatex.com

Clear Profit
Tel: +44 1273 311 289
E-mail: mail@clear-profit.com
Web: http://www.clear-profit.com

Climate Change Corp
Ethical Corporation
7-9 Fashion Street
London
E1 6PX
United Kingdom
Tel: + 44 207 375 7183
E-mail. editor@climatechangecorp.com
Web: http://www.climatechangecorp.com

Climate Savers Computing Initiative
Tel: (503) 619-0655
Web: http://www.climatesaverscomputing.org

**Coalition for Environmentally Responsible Economies (CERES)
Principles**
99 Chauncy Street, 6th Floor
Boston, MA 02111
USA
Phone: (617) 247-0700
Fax: (617) 267-5400
E-mail: fleming@ceres.org
Web: http://www.ceres.org/page.aspx?pid=705

Common Codes for the Coffee Community
4C Secretariat
Adenauerallee 108
53113 Bonn
Germany
Phone: +49 228 850 50 0
Fax: +49 228 850 60 20
E-mail: info@4c-coffeeassociation.org
Web: http://www.4c-coffeeassociation.org

Computer Professionals for Social Responsibility
PO Box 20046
Stanford, CA 94309-0046
USA
Tel: (650) 989-1294
E-mail: office@cpsr.org
Web: http://cpsr.org

Consortium for Green Design and Manufacturing (CGDM)
University of California
1115 Etcheverry Hall
Berkeley, CA 94720-1740
USA
Tel: (510) 642-8657
E-mail: cgdm@newton.berkeley.com
Web: http://cgdm.berkeley.edu

Cool Air-Clean Planet
100 Market Street, Suite 204
Portsmouth, NH 03801
USA
Tel: (603) 422-6464
Fax: (603) 422-6441
E-mail: info@cleanair-coolplanet.org
Web: http://www.cleanair-coolplanet.org

Corporate Knights
215 Spadina Avenue, Suite 121
Toronto, ON M5T 2C7
Canada

Tel: (416) 203-4674
Fax: (416) 979-3936
E-mail: info@corporateknights.ca
Web: http://www.corporteknights.ca

Corporate Responsibility Index

St. James Ethics Centre
GPO Box 3599
Sydney NSW 2001
Australia
Tel: +61 2 9299 9566
Fax: +61 2 9299 9477
E-mail: cr-index@ethics.org.au
Web: http://www.corporate-responsibility.com.au

Corporate Responsibility Index

Business in the Community
137 Shepherdess Walk
London N1 7RQ
United Kingdom
Tel: +4420 7566 8650
E-mail: information@bitc.org.uk
Web: http://www.bitc.org.uk

Corporate Responsibility Officer (CRO) Magazine

343 Thornall Street, Suite 515
Edison, NJ 08837-2206
USA
Tel: (732) 476-6160
Fax: (732) 476-6155
Web: http://www.thecro.com

Cradle to Cradle Design and Certification

McDonough Braungart Design Chemistry, LLC (MBDC)
1001 East Market Street, Suite 200
Charlottesville, VA 22902
USA
Tel: (434) 295-1111
Fax: (434) 295-1500

E-mail: info@mbdc.com
Web: http://www.mbdc.com/c2c_home.htm

Crowdspring.com
Web: http://www.crowdspring.com

CSRwire
Meadowbrook Lane Capital, LLC
250 Albany Street
Springfield, MA 01101-5496
USA
Tel: (802) 251-0110
E-mail: help@csrwire.com
Web: http://www.csrwire.com

Diplomats Without Borders/Diplomates sans Frontières
Rue Marignac 5
1206 Genève
SUISSE
Tel: +41 22 347 38 09
Fax: +41 22 347 38 16
E-mail: geneva@dsf-dwb.org
Web: http://www.diplomatswithoutborders.org

Domini 400 Social Index
KLD Research & Analytics, Inc.
121 High Street, 4th Floor
Boston, MA 02110
USA
Tel: (617) 426-5270
Fax: (617) 426-5299
E-mail: info@kld.com
http://www.kld.com/indexes/ds400index/index.html

Domini Social Investments
PO Box 9785
Providence, RI 02940
USA

Tel: (212) 217-1112
Fax: (212) 217-1101
E-mail: kshaprio@domini.com
Web: http://www.domini.com

Dow Jones Sustainability Indexes
SAM Indexes GmbH
Josefstrasse 218
8005 Zurich
Switzerland
Tel: +41 44 653 1802
Fax: +41 44 653 1810
E-mail: indexes@sam-group.com
Web: http://www.sustainability-index.com

EcoButton
E-mail: enquiries@eco-button.com
Web: http://www.eco-button.com/usa/A2.0.business.htm

EcoLogo
c/o TerraChoice Environmental Marketing
2 Penn Center Plaza, Suite 200
Philadelphia, PA 19102
USA
Tel: (800) 478-0399
Fax: (613) 247-2228
E-mail: ecologo@terrachoice.com
Web: http://www.ecologo.org/en

Electronic Product Environmental Assessment Tool (EPEAT)
Environmental Protection Agency
Sarah O'Brien
EPEAT Outreach Director
Tel: (802) 479-0317
E-mail: sarah.obrien@greenelectronicscouncil.org
Web: http://www.epeat.net

EmpXtrack
EmpXtrack Division
Saigun Technologies
134 N. Manchester Lane
Bloomingdale, IL 60108
USA
Tel: (888) 840-2682
Fax: (866) 825-3204
E-mail: marketing@empxtrack.com
Web: http://www.empxtrack.com

ENERGY STAR
U.S. Environmental Protection Agency
U.S. Department of Energy
1200 Pennsylvania Avenue NW
Washington, DC 20460
USA
Tel: (888) 782-7937
Web: http://www.energystar.gov

EnerSure
TrendPoint Systems, LLC
111 Deerwood Road, Suite 200
San Ramon, CA 94583
USA
Tel: (925) 855-0600
E-mail: info@trendpoint.com
Web: http://enersure.com

Enterprise for a Sustainable World
321 Main Street, Suite 201
Ann Arbor, MI 48104
USA
Tel: (734) 369-8060
Web: http://www.e4sw.org

EnviroCube
TrendPoint Systems, LLC
111 Deerwood Road, Suite 200
San Ramon, CA 94583
USA
Tel: (925) 855-0600
E-mail: info@trendpoint.com
Web: http://enersure.com

Environmental Leader
123 North College Avenue, Suite 200
Fort Collins, CO 80524
USA
Tel: (970) 215-1996
E-mail: publisher@environmentalleader.com
Web: http://www.environmentalleader.com

Environmental News Network
402 North B Street
Fairfield, IA 52556
USA
Tel: (641) 472-2790
Fax: (641) 481-2795
Web: http://www.enn.com

Equator Principles
E-mail: secretariat@equator-principles.com
Web: http://www.equator-principles.com/index.shtml

Erb Institute for Global Sustainable Enterprise (Erb)
University of Michigan
440 Church Street, Dana Building
Ann Arbor, MI 48109-1041
USA
Fax: (734) 647-8551
E-mail: erbinstitute@umich.edu
Web: http://www.erb.umich.edu

Ethical Corporation
7-9 Fashion Street
London
E1 6PX
United Kingdom
Tel: +44 20 73 75 7213
E-mail: editor@ethicalcorp.com
Web: http://www.ethicalcorp.com

Ethical Investment Research Service
80-84 Bondway
London
SW8 1SF
United Kingdom
Tel: +44 20 7840 5700
Fax: +44 20 7735 5323
E-mail: ethics@eiris.org
Web: http://www.eiris.org/index.htm

Ethical Trading Initiative
8 Coldbath Square
London
EC1R 5HL
United Kingdom
Phone: +44 20 7841 4350
Fax: +44 20 7833 1569
Tel: eti@eti.org.uk
Web: http://www.ethicaltrade.org/Z/home/index.shtml

European Commission Code of Conduct for Green Data Centers
European Commission—JRC
TP 450
I-21020 Ispra (VA)
ITALY
Tel: +39 0332 78 9299
Fax: +39 0332 78 9992
Web: http://re.jrc.ec.europa.eu/energyefficiency/html/standby_initiative
    _data%20centers.htm

European Union Emissions Trading Scheme
European Commission
Environment DG
B–1049 Brussels
Belgium
Web: http://ec.europa.eu/environment/climat/emission/index_en.htm

Extractive Industries Transparency Initiative
EITI International Secretariat
Ruselokkveien 26
0251 Oslo
Norway
Tel: +47 2224 2105
Fax: +47 2224 2115
E-mail: secretariat@eitransparency.org
Web: http://eitransparency.org/contact

Fair Labor Association
1707 L Street NW, Suite 200
Washington, DC 20036
USA
Tel: (202) 898-1000
Fax: (866) 649-0624
E-mail: info@fairlabor.org
Web: http://www.fairlabor.org

Fair Trade Federation
Hecker Center, Suite 107
3025 Fourth Street NE
Washington, DC 20017-1102
USA
Tel: (202) 636-3547
Fax: (202) 636-3549
E-mail: info@FairTradeFederation.org
Web: http://www.fairtradefederation.org/ht/d/sp/i/185/pid/185

Federal Trade Commission's (FTC) Green Guides
600 Pennsylvania Avenue NW
Washington, DC 20580
USA

Tel: (202) 326-2222

Web:http://ecfr.gpoaccess.gov/cgi/t/text/text-idx?c=ecfr&sid=b2333ddf9
6abf25788ef3037ffcfb40a&tpl=/ecfrbrowse/Title16/16cfr260_main
_02.tpl

FellowForce

Soestdijkerstraatweg 27B
1213 VR Hilversum
The Netherlands
Kvk number: 32 12 31 23
E-mail: customerservice@fellowforce.com
Web: http://www.fellowforce.com

Financial Services Volunteer Corps

FSVC New York
800 3rd Avenue, 11th Floor
New York, NY 10022
USA
Tel: (212) 771-1400
Fax: (212) 771-1463
Web: http://www.fsvc.org

Forest Stewardship Council (FSC)

212 Third Avenue North, Suite 280
Minneapolis, MN 55401
USA
Tel: (612) 353-4511
Fax: (612) 208-1565
E-mail: info@fscus.org
Web: http://www.fscus.org

Forum for Corporate Sustainability Management (CSM)

IMD
Ch. De Bellerive 23
P.O. Box 915
Ch-1001 Lausanne
Switzerland
Tel: +41 21 618 0111
Fax: +41 21 618 0707
Web: http://www.imd.ch/research/centers/csm/index.cfm

Freecycle Network, The
Web: http://www.freecycle.org

FTSE4Good Index
FTSE Americas, Inc.
1330 Avenue of the Americas, 10th Floor
New York, NY 10019
USA
Tel: (212) 641-6124
E-mail: info@ftse.com
Web: http://www.ftse.com/Indices/FTSE4Good_Index_Series/index.jsp

Geek Corps
1900 M Street NW, Suite 500
Washington, DC 20036
USA
Tel: (202) 326-0280
E-mail: geekcorps@iesc.org
Web: http://www.geekcorps.org

Global Environmental Management Initiative
1155 15th Street NW, Suite 500
Washington, DC 20005
USA
Tel: (202) 296-7449
Fax: (202) 296-7442
Web: http://www.gemi.org/gemihome.aspx

Global Environmental Management Initiative Water Tool
Global Exchange
2017 Mission Street, Suite 303
San Francisco, CA 94110
USA
Tel: (415) 255-7296
Web: http://www.discoverthenetworks.org/groupProfile.asp?grpid=6151

Global eSustainability Initiative
GeSI Secretariat
c/o Scotland House
Rond Point Schuman 6
B-1040 Brussels
Belgium
Tel: +32 2 282 84 42
Fax: +32 2 282 84 14
E-mail: info@gesi.org
Web: http://www.gesi.org

Global Exchange
2017 Mission Street, 2nd Floor
San Francisco, CA 94110
USA
Tel: (415) 255-7296
Fax: (415) 255-7498
Web: http://www.globalexchange.org

Global Institute of Sustainability
Arizona State University
PO Box 875402
Tempe, AZ 85287-5402
USA
Tel: (480) 965-2975
Fax: (480) 965-8087
E-mail: sustainability@asu.edu
Web: http://sustainability.asu.edu

Global Reporting Initiative (GRI)
PO Box 10039
1001 EA
Amsterdam, The Netherlands
Tel: +31 20 531 00 00
Fax: +31 20 531 00 31
Web: http://www.globalreporting.org/Home

Global Sullivan Principles
Leon H. Sullivan Foundation
1800 K Street NW, Suite 1021
Washington, DC 20006
USA
Tel: (202) 736-2239
Fax: (202) 736-2226
E-mail: thegsp@thesullivanfoundation.org
Web: http://www.thesullivanfoundation.org/gsp/default.asp

Global Water Tool
American Society of Civil Engineers
Committee on Critical Infrastructure
101 Constitution Avenue NW, Suite 375 East
Washington, DC 20001
USA
Tel: (202) 789-7853
E-mail: cci@asce.org
Web: http://ciasce.asce.org/news-article/global-water-tool

GOOD Magazine
GOOD Worldwide, Inc.
6824 Melrose Avenue
Los Angeles, CA 90038
USA
Tel: (310) 691-1020
Fax: (310) 691-1033
E-mail: hello@goodinc.com
Web: http://www.good.is

GoToMeeting.com
Citrix Online Headquarters
Division of Citrix Systems
6500 Hollister Avenue
Goleta, CA 93117
USA
Tel: (805) 690-6400
Fax: (805) 690-6471

E-mail: info@citrixonline.com
Web: https://www2.gotowebinar.com/en_US/webinar/entry/entry.tmpl

GoToWebinar.com

Citrix Online Headquarters
Division of Citrix Systems
6500 Hollister Avenue
Goleta, CA 93117
USA
Tel: (805) 690-6400
Fax: (805) 690-6471
E-mail: info@citrixonline.com
Web: https://www1.gotomeeting.com/?Portal=www.gotomeeting.com

Green for All

1611 Telegraph Avenue, Suite 600
Oakland, CA 94612
USA
Tel: (510) 663-6500
E-mail: info@greenforall.org
Web: http://www.greenforall.org

Green Computing Impact Organization

Green Computing Impact Organization
140 Kendrick Street, Building A, Suite 300
Needham, MA 02494
USA
Tel: (781) 444-0404
Fax: (781) 444-0320
E-mail: info@omg.org
Web: http://www.omg.org/news/releases/pr2008/12-11-08.htm

Green Computing Maturity Model Process

Green Computing Impact Organization
140 Kendrick Street, Building A, Suite 300
Needham, MA 02494
USA
Tel: (781) 444-0404
Fax: (781) 444-0320

E-mail: info@gcio.org
Web: http://www.gcio.org/vendors.html

Green Design Institute (GDI)
Michael Griffin, Executive Director
Green Design Institute
Carnegie Mellon University
5000 Forbes Avenue
Pittsburgh, PA 15213-3890
USA
Tel: (412) 268-2299
E-mail: green-design@andrew.cmu.edu
Web: http://www.ce.cmu.edu/GreenDesign

Green Electronics Council
One World Trade Center
121 SW Salmon Street, Suite 210
Portland, OR 97204
USA
Tel: (503) 279-9383
E-mail: info@greenelectronicscouncil.org
Web: http://www.greenelectronicscouncil.org

Green Grid, The
3855 SW 153rd Drive
Beaverton, OR 97006
USA
Tel: (503) 619-0653
Fax: (503) 644-6708
E-mail: admin@lists.thegreengrid.org
Web: http://www.thegreengrid.org/home

Green ICT Strategies Course
Australian Computer Society
Level 3, 160 Clarence Street
Sydney NSW 2000
Australia
Tel: +61 2 9299 3666
Fax: +61 2 9299 3997

E-mail: info@acs.org.au

Web: http://www.acs.org.au/cpeprogram/index.cfm?action=show&conID
=greenict

Green Power Partnership

U.S. Environmental Protection Agency

Web: http://www.epa.gov/greenpower

Green Seal

1001 Connecticut Avenue NW, Suite 827

Washington, DC 20036-5525

USA

Tel: (202) 872-6400

Fax: (202) 872-4324

E-mail: greenseal@greenseal.org

Web: http://www.greenseal.org

GreenBiz

Greener World Media

405 14th Street, Suite 1414

Oakland, CA 94612

USA

Tel: (510) 550-8285

E-mail: info@greenerworldmedia.com

Web: http://www.greenbiz.com

GreenDreamJobs

E-mail: info@sustainablebusiness.com

Web: http://www.sustainablebusiness.com/index.cfm/go/greendreamjobs
.main

Greener Computing

405 14th Street, Suite 1414

Oakland, CA 94612

USA

Tel: (510) 550-8285

E-mail: editor@greenerworldmedia.com

Web: http://www.ecosherpa.com

Greener World Media
405 14th Street, Suite 1414
Oakland, CA 94612
USA
Tel: (510) 550-8285
E-mail: info@greenerworldmedia.com
Web: http://www.greenerworldmedia.com/index.html

Greenhouse Gas (GHG) Protocol
World Resources Institute
10 G Street NE, Suite 800
Washington, DC 20002
USA
World Business Council for Sustainable Development
4, Chemin de Conches
CH-1231 Conches-Geneva
Switzerland
Web: http://www.ghgprotocol.org

GreenJobInterview.com
20311 SW Acacia, Suite 240
Newport Beach, CA 92660
USA
Tel: (888) 838-8331, ext. 200
Fax: (949) 553-8330
E-mail: support@greenjobinterview.com
Web: http://www.greenjobinterview.com

GreenMoney Journal
PO Box 67
Santa Fe, NM 87504
USA
Tel: (505) 988-7423
E-mail: info@greenmoneyjournal.com
Web: http://www.greenmoneyjournal.com

Grist Magazine
710 Second Avenue, Suite 860
Seattle, WA 98104
USA

Tel: (206) 876-2020
Fax: (253) 423-6487
E-mail: grist@grist.org
Web: http://www.grist.org

Halogen eAppraisal
Tel: (866) 270-8409
E-mail: info@halogensoftware.com
Web: http://www.halogensoftware.com/products/halogen-eappraisal

HR.com
124 Wellington Street East
Aurora, Ontario
Canada
L4G 1J1
Tel: (877) 472-6648
E-mail: info@hr.com
Web: http://www.hr.com

Human Rights Watch
350 Fifth Avenue, 34th floor
New York, NY 10118-3299
USA
Tel: (212) 290-4700
Fax: (212) 736-1300
Web: http://www.hrw.org

Idealist
302 Fifth Avenue, 11th Floor
New York, NY 10001
USA
Tel: (212) 843-3973
Fax: (212) 695-7243
Web: http://www.idealist.org

InnoCentive
201 Jones Road, 4th Floor East
Waltham, MA 02451
USA

Phone: (978) 482-3300
Fax: (978) 482-3400
Web: http://www.innocentive.com

Innovation Exchange

2 Berkeley Street, Suite 300
Toronto, Ontario
M5A 2W3
Canada
Tel: (416) 214-4840
E-mail: info@innovationexchange.com
Web: http://www.innovationexchange.com

Interfaith Center on Corporate Responsibility

475 Riverside Drive, Room 1842
New York, NY 10115
USA
Tel: (212) 870-2295
Fax: (212) 870-2023
E-mail: info@iccr.org
Web: http://www.iccr.org

Intergovernmental Panel on Climate Change

IPCC Secretariat
C/O World Meteorological Organization
7bis Avenue de la Paix, C.P. 2300
CH-1211 Geneva 2
Switzerland
Tel: +41 22 730 8208/84
Fax: +41 22 730 8025
E-mail: IPCC-Sec@wmo.int
Web: http://www.ipcc.ch/index.htm

International Chamber of Commerce Business Charter for Sustainable Development

International Chamber of Commerce
38 cours Albert 1er
75008 Paris
France

Tel: +33 1 49 53 28 28
Fax: +33 1 49 53 28 59
Web: http://www.iccmex.org.mx/intranet/documentos/CHARTER.pdf

International Executive Service Corps
1900 M Street NW, Suite 500
Washington, DC 20036
USA
Tel: (202) 326-0280
Fax: (202) 326-0289
E-mail: iesc@iesc.org
Web: http://www.iesc.org

International Federation of Accountants
545 Fifth Avenue, 14th Floor
New York, NY 10017
USA
Tel: (212) 286-9344
Fax: (212) 286-9570
Web: http://www.ifac.org

International Finance Corporation (IFC) Performance Standards
2121 Pennsylvania Avenue, NW
Washington, DC 20433
USA
Tel: (202) 473-3800
Fax: (202) 974-4384
Web: http://www.ifc.org/ifcext/enviro.nsf/Content/PerformanceStandards

International Labor Rights Forum
2001 S Street NW #420
Washington, DC 20009
USA
Tel: (202) 347-4100
Fax: (202) 347-4885
E-mail: laborrights@ilrf.org
Web: http://www.laborrights.org

International Labour Organization
4 route des Morillons
CH-1211 Genève 22
Switzerland
Tel: +41 22 799 6111
Fax: +41 22 798 8685
E-mail: ilo@ilo.org
Web: http://www.ilo.org

International Labour Standards
International Labour Organization
4 route des Morillons
CH-1211 Genève 22
Switzerland
Tel: +41 22 799 6111
Fax: +41 22 798 8685
E-mail: ilo@ilo.org
Web: http://www.ilo.org/global/What_we_do/InternationalLabourStandards/
    lang-en/index.htm

International Organization for Standardization (ISO)
1, ch. de la Voie-Creuse
Case postale 56
CH-1211 Geneva 20
Switzerland
Tel: +41 22 749 01 11
Fax: +41 22 733 34 30
Web: http://www.iso.ch

**International Standard on Assurance Engagements (ISAE) 3000
Standard**
1620 W. Fountainhead Parkway, Suite 100
Tempe, AZ 85282
USA
Tel: (480) 346-5500
Fax: (480) 346-5599
Web: http://www.ess-home.com/regs/isae-3000.aspx

International Sustainability Professionals Society
2515 Northeast 17th Avenue, Suite 300
Portland, OR 97212
USA
Web: http://sustainabilityprofessionals.org/

Investor Responsibility Research Center
1350 Connecticut Avenue Northwest
Washington, DC 20036-1722
USA
Tel: (202) 833-0700
Web: http://www.irrc.org

KLD Indexes
KLD Research & Analytics, Inc.
121 High Street, 4th Floor
Boston, MA 02110
USA
Tel: (617) 502-6737
E-mail: indexes@kld.com
Web: http://www.kld.com/indexes/index.html

Kyoto Protocol
United Nations Framework Convention on Climate Change
Haus Carstanjen
Martin-Luther-King-Strasse 8
53175 Bonn
Germany
Tel: +49 228 815 1000
Fax: +49 228 815 1999
Web: http://unfccc.int/kyoto_protocol/items/2830.php

LEED (Leadership in Energy and Environmental Design)
U.S. Green Building Council
1800 Massachusetts Avenue NW, Suite 300
Washington, DC 20036
USA

Tel: (202) 742-3792
Fax: (202) 828-5110
Web: http://www.usgbc.org

Life Cycle Assessment
Attn: Thomas Gloria, Ph.D.
Web: http://www.life-cycle.org/LCA_soft.htm

LOHAS Journal
833 W. South Boulder Road
Louisville, CO 80027
USA
Tel: (303) 222-8283
Fax: (303) 222-8250
E-mail: info@lohas.com
Web: http://www.lohas.com

Matter of Trust
99 St. Germain Avenue
San Francisco, CA 94114
USA
Tel: (415) 242-6041
E-mail: team@matteroftrust.org
Web: http://matteroftrust.org

Matter Network
555 Post Street
San Francisco, CA 94102
USA
Tel: (415) 367-9420
Web: http://www.matternetwork.com

MBA-Nonprofit Connection
PO Box 640
Palo Alto, CA 94302
USA
Tel: (650) 323-9639
E-mail: partnership@mnconnection.org
Web: http://www.mnconnection.org

MBAs Without Borders
136 Trafalgar Road
Oakville, Ontario L6J 3G5
Canada
Tel: (613) 482-9483
Fax: (416) 849-0101
E-mail: info@mbaswithoutborders.org
Web: http://mbaswithoutborders.org

Measuring Impact Framework
World Business Council for Sustainable Development
Development Focus Area
4, chemin de Conches
1231 Conches-Geneva
Switzerland
Tel: +41 22 839 3192
Fax: +41 22 839 3131
E-mail: info@wbcsd.org
Web: www.wbcsd.org/web/measuringimpact.htm

Midwestern Greenhouse Gas Reduction Accord
444 North Capitol Street NW, Suite 401
Washington, DC 20001
USA
Tel: (202) 624-5460
Fax: (202) 624-5452
Web: http://www.midwesternaccord.org

Minnesota Center for Corporate Responsibility
University of St. Thomas
1000 LaSalle Avenue, Suite 153
Minneapolis, MN 55403
USA
Tel: (651) 962-4120
Fax: (651) 962-4125
E-mail: mccr_ust@stthomas.edu
Web: http://www.mbbnet.umn.edu/associations/mccr.html

Mother Jones Earth
222 Sutter Street, Suite 600
San Francisco, CA 94108
USA
Tel: (415) 321-1700
Web: http://www.motherjones.com

National Association of Socially Responsible Organizations
643 Moody Street, 2nd Floor
Waltham, MA 02453
USA
Tel: (781) 893-4343
Fax: (800) 562-8588
E-mail: info@nasro-co-op.com
Web: http://www.nasro-co-op.com

Natural Step, The
Sveavägen 98, 5th floor
SE-113 50 Stockholm
Sweden
Tel: +46 8 789 29 00
Fax: +46 8 789 29 39
E-mail: info@thenaturalstep.org
Web: http://www.naturalstep.org

NEED Magazine
2303 Kennedy Street NE, Suite 502
Minneapolis, MN 55413
USA
Tel: (612) 379-4025
Fax: (612) 379-4033
E-mail: info@needmagazine.com
Web: http://www.needmagazine.com

Net Impact
88 First Street, Suite 200
San Francisco, CA 94105
USA

Tel: (415) 495-4230
Fax: (415) 495-4229
E-mail: info@netimpact.org
Web: http://netimpact.org

New South Wales Greenhouse Gas Reduction Scheme
Greenhouse Gas Reduction Scheme Administrator
PO Box Q290
QVB POST OFFICE NSW 1230
Australia
Tel: +61 02 9290 8452
Web: http://www.greenhousegas.nsw.gov.au

New Ventures
World Resources Institute
Markets & Enterprise Program
10 G Street NE Suite 800
Washington, DC 20002
USA
Tel: (202) 729-7669
E-mail: slall@wri.org
Web: http://www.new-ventures.org

New Zealand Emissions Trading Scheme
PO Box 10362
Wellington 6143
New Zealand
Tel: +64 4 439 7400
Fax: + 64 4 439 7700
E-mail: information@mfe.govt.nz
Web:http://www.climatechange.govt.nz/emissions-trading-scheme/index
    .html

NineSigma
Home Office:
NineSigma, Inc.
23611 Chagrin Blvd., Suite 320
Cleveland, OH 44122-5540
USA

Tel: (216) 295-4800
Fax: (216) 295-4825
E-mail: sales@ninesigma.com
Europe:
NineSigma Europe BVBA
Koning Leopold I straat 3
B-3000 Leuven
Belgium
Tel: +32 24 42 08
Fax: +32 24 42 89
E-mail: zynga@ninesigma.com
Asia:
NineSigma Japan, Inc.
Kandaogawamachi Tosei, Building 2, 7th Floor
3-3 Kandaogawamachi, Chiyoda-ku
Tokyo, 101-0052 Japan
Tel: +81 3 3219 2001
Fax: +81 3 3219 2008
E-mail: suwa@ninesigma.com
Web: http://www.ninesigma.com

Northwest Earth Institute
317 SW Alder, Suite 1050
Portland, OR 97204
USA
Tel: (503) 227-2807
Fax: (503) 227-2917
E-mail: contact@nwei.org
Web: http://www.nwei.org

OHSAS 18001
Occupational Health & Safety Group
OHS House
Macclesfield
SK10 7NZ
Cheshire
United Kingdom

Web: http://www.ohsas-18001-occupational-health-and-safety.com/ohsas
-18001-kit.htm
http://www.standardsdirect.org/ohsas.htm

Organization for Economic Cooperation and Development
Principles of Corporate Governance
2, rue André Pascal
F-75775 Paris Cedex 16
France
Tel: +33 1 45 24 82 00
Fax: +33 1 45 24 85 00
Web: http://www.oecd.org/document/49/0,3343,en_2649_34813_31530865
_1_1_1_37439,00.html

Peace Through Commerce
Jeff Klein, Executive Director and Chief Activation Officer
FLOW, Inc.
1510 Falcon Ledge Drive
Austin, TX 78746
USA
Tel: (415) 497-0996
E-mail: jeff@flowidealism.org
Web: http://www.peacethroughcommerce.com

Plenty Magazine
250 West 49th Street, Suite 403
New York, NY 10019
USA
Tel: (212) 757-3447
Fax: (212) 757-3799
E-mail: info@plentymag.com
Web: http://www.plentymag.com

Regional Greenhouse Gas Initiative, Inc. (RGGI)
90 Church Street, 4th Floor
New York, NY 10007
USA
Tel: (212) 417-7327
Web: http://www.rggi.org/home

Responsible Care
International Council of Chemical Associations (ICCA) c/o ACC
1300 Wilson Blvd.
Arlington, VA 22209
USA
Web: http://www.responsiblecare.org

RugMark Foundation
2001 S Street NW, Suite 430
Washington, DC 20009
USA
Tel: (202) 234-9050
Fax: (202) 347-4885
E-mail: Info@RugMark.org
Web: http://www.rugmark.org

SA8000
Social Accountability International
15 West 44th Street, 6th Floor
New York, NY 10036
USA
Tel: (212) 684-1414
Fax: (212) 684-1515
E-mail: info@sa-intl.org
Web: http://www.sa-intl.org/index.cfm?fuseaction=Page.viewPage&pageId
    =473

Salary.com
Corporate Headquarters
195 West Street
Waltham, MA 02451-1111
USA
Tel: (866) 725-2791
Web: http://salary.com

SalarySource.com
HR Answers, Inc.
7659 SW Mohawk Street
Tualatin, OR 97062
USA
Tel: (877) 287-4476
Fax: (503) 692-3772
E-mail: service@salarysource.com
Web: http://salarysource.com

SIGMA Project
C/O British Standards Institution
389 Chiswick High Road
London W 44AL
United Kingdom
Tel: +44 20 8996 7662
Fax: +44 20 8996 7400
E-mail: Tim.Sunderland@bsi-global.com
Web: http://www.projectsigma.co.uk/Toolkit/SustainabilityAccountingGuide
.asp

Social Accountability International
15 West 44th Street, 6th Floor
New York, NY 10036
USA
Tel: (212) 684-1414
Fax: (212) 684-1515
E-mail: info@sa-intl.org
Web: http://www.sa-intl.org

Social Investment Forum
910 17th Street NW, Suite 1000
Washington, DC 20006
USA
Tel: (202) 872-5359
E-mail: rmacknight@socialinvest.org
http://www.socialinvest.org

Social Venture Network
PO Box 29221
San Francisco, CA 94129
USA
Tel: (415) 561-6501
E-mail: svn@svn.org
Web: http://www.svn.org

Stakeholder Engagement Manual
AccountAbility
250-252 Goswell Road
London
EC1V 7EB
United Kingdom
Tel: +44 20 7549 0400
Fax: +44 20 7253 74400
250 24th Street NW, Suite 300
Washington, DC 20037
USA
Tel: (202) 835-1692
Fax: (202) 835-1693
E-mail: secretariat@accountability21.net
Web: http://www.accountability21.net/uploadedFiles/publications/
    Stakeholder%20Engagement%20Handbook.pdf

Stakeholder Engagement Standard
AccountAbility
250-252 Goswell Road
London
EC1V 7EB
United Kingdom
Tel: +44 20 7549 0400
Fax: +44 20 7253 74400

250 24th Street NW, Suite 300
Washington, DC 20037
USA
Tel: (202) 835-1692
Fax: (202) 835-1693
E-mail: secretariat@accountability21.net
Web: http://www.accountability21.net/uploadedFiles/publications/
    SES%20Exposure%20Draft%20-%20FullPDF.pdf

Standards of Excellence in Corporate Community Involvement
Boston College Center for Corporate Citizenship
Carroll School of Management
55 Lee Road
Chestnut Hill, MA 02467-3942
USA
Tel: (617) 552-4545
Fax: (617) 552+8499
E-mail: ccc@bc.edu
Web: http://www.bcccc.net/index.cfm?fuseaction=Page.viewPage&pageID
    =707

Stopdodo.com
St John's Courtyard BCM 4675
London
WC1N 3XX
United Kingdom
Contact: Mr. Ad Davids
E-mail: ad@stopdodo.com
North America:
ECM #79253
93 S. Jackson Street
Seattle, Washington 98104-2818
USA
Contact: Ms. Janey Marks
E-mail: janey@stopdodo.com

Europe:
28 Calle de la Iglesia
Carratraca
Spain
Contact: Snr. Victor Banares
E-mail: victor@stopdodo.com
Web: http://www.stopdodo.com

Sustainability Assurance Practitioner

AccountAbility
250-252 Goswell Road
London
EC1V 7EB
UK
Tel: +44 20 7549 0400
Fax: +44 20 7253 74400
250 24th Street NW, Suite 300
Washington, DC 20037
USA
Tel: (202) 835-1692
Fax: (202) 835-1693
E-mail: secretariat@accountability21.net
Web: http://www.irca.org/certification/certification_11.html

Sustainable Industries

230 California Street, Suite 410
San Francisco, CA 94111
USA
Tel: (415) 762-3941
Fax: (415) 762-3945
E-mail: brian@sustainableindustries.com
Web: http://www.sustainableindustries.com

Sustainable Investment Research International (SiRi) Network
SiRi Company Ltd.
Philippe Spicher, Managing Director
c/o Centre Info SA
Rue de Romont 2
CH-1700 Fribourg
Switzerland
E-mail: philippe.spicher@centreinfo.ch
Web: http://www.siricompany.com

Sweatshop Watch
1250 So. Los Angeles Street, Suite 212
Los Angeles, CA 90015
USA
Tel: (213) 748-5945
Fax: (213) 748-5955
E-mail: sweatinfo@sweatshopwatch.org
Web: http://www.sweatshopwatch.org

Taproot Foundation
466 Geary Street, Suite 200
San Francisco, CA 94102
USA
Tel: (415) 359-1423
E-mail: national@taprootfoundation.org
Web: http://www.taprootfoundation.org

TeamMBA
Graduate Management Admission Council
Attention: Chief Privacy Official
1600 Tysons Boulevard, Suite 1400
McLean, VA 22102
USA
Tel: (703) 245-4343
E-mail: teammba@gmac.com
Web: http://www.gmac.com/teammba

TechnoServ
PO Box 2240
Manama
Kingdom of Bahrain
Tel: +973 17 712443
Fax: +973 17 713627
E-mail: info@techno-serv.com
Web: http://www.techno-serv.com

Transparency International
Alt-Moabit 96
10559 Berlin
Germany
Tel: +49 30 3438 20 0
Fax: +49 30 3470 3912
E-mail: ti@transparency.org
Web: http://www.transparency.org

TreeHugger
Discovery Communications, LLC
Web: http://www.treehugger.com

Triple Pundit
Web: http://www.triplepundit.com

United Nations
One United Nations Plaza
New York, NY 10017
USA
Tel: (917) 679-8144
Fax: (212) 963-1207
E-mail: powerg@un.org
Web: http://www.unglobalcompact.org

United Nations Millennium Development Goals
United Nations Development Programme
One United Nations Plaza
New York, NY 10017
USA

Tel: (212) 906-5000
Fax: (212) 906-5364
E-mail: ohr.recruitment.hq@undp.org
Web: http://www.un.org/millenniumgoals

United Nations Human Rights Norms for Business
United Nations Centre for Human Rights
United Nations Office at Geneva
8-14 Avenue de la Paix
1211 Geneva 10
Switzerland
Tel.: +41 22 917 3924
Fax: +41 22 917 0213
Web: http://www.un.org/rights/dpi1774e.htm
Web: http://www.unhchr.ch/huridocda/huridoca.nsf/(Symbol)/E.CN.4
    .Sub.2.2003.12.Rev.2.En

U.S. Green Building Council (USGBC)
1800 Massachusetts Avenue NW, Suite 300
Washington, DC 20036
USA
Tel: (202) 742-3792
Fax: (202) 828-5110
Web: http://www.usgbc.org

Verdiem
1601 2nd Avenue, Suite 701
Seattle, WA 98101
USA
Tel: (206) 838-2800
Fax: (206) 838-2801
Web: http://www.verdiem.com

Verite
44 Belchertown Road
Amherst, MA 01002
USA
Tel: (413) 253-9227
Fax: (413) 256-8960

E-mail: verite@verite.org
Web: http://www.verite.org

Wall Street Without Walls
1720 N Street NW
Washington, DC 20036
USA
Tel: (202) 375-7762
Fax: (202) 375-7761
E-mail: john.nelson@wallstreetwithoutwalls.com
Web: http://www.wallstreetwithoutwalls.com

Western Climate Initiative
Patrick Cummins, Project Manager, Western Governors' Association
Tel: (970) 884-4770
E-mail: pcummins@westgov.org
Web: http://www.westernclimateinitiative.org

Wolfsberg Trade Finance Principles
The Wolfsberg Group
Telecom & Network Sery, Bahnhofstr. 45
Zurich, zh8098
Switzerland
Tel: +41 1 234 1111
Fax: +41 1 236 7634
E-mail: info@wolfsberg-principles.com
Web: http://www.wolfsberg-principles.com

World Business Council for Sustainable Development (WBCSD)
4, chemin de Conches
1231 Conches-Geneva
Switzerland
Tel: +41 22 839 3100
Fax: +41 22 839 3131
1744 R Street NW
Washington, DC 20009
USA
Tel: (202) 420-7745
Fax: (202) 265-1662

E-mail: info@wbcsd.org
Web: http://wbcsd.org

World Resources Institute (WRI)
10 G Street NE, Suite 800
Washington, DC 20002
USA
Tel: (202) 729-7600
Fax: (202) 729-7610
E-mail: abutler@wri.org
Web: http://www.wri.org

Yet2.com
North America:
10 Kearney Road, Suite 300
Needham, MA 02494
USA
Tel: (781) 972-0600
Fax: (781) 972-0601
E-mail: americas@yet2.com
Europe:
Liverpool Science Park
Innovation Centre
131 Mount Pleasant
Liverpool, L3 5TF
United Kingdom
Tel: +44 151 705 3539
Fax: + 44 151 705 3542
E-mail: europe@yet2.com
Asia:
2F Kawasaki Park, Bldg. I
3-15-5, Kanda Nishiki-cho
Chiyoda-ku, Tokyo, 101-0054
Japan
Tel: +81 3 5217 0217
Fax: +81 3 5217 0218
E-mail: japan@yet2.com
E-mail for all: info@yet2.com
Web: http://www.yet2.com/app/about/home

Zero Waste Alliance
One World Trade Center
121 SW Salmon Street, Suite 210
Portland, OR 97204
USA
Tel: (503) 279-9383
Fax: (503) 279-9381
E-mail: info@zerowaste.org
Web: http://www.zerowaste.org/index.htm

Notes

Chapter 1

1. Brundtland (1987).
2. Brundtland (1987).

Chapter 2

1. Elkington (1997).
2. Obama for America (2007).
3. Gardner (2008).
4. Kollmuss and Bowell (2007).
5. Clean Air-Cool Planet (2006).
6. Wal-Mart Stores, Inc. (2008a).
7. Wal-Mart Stores, Inc. (2008a).
8. Wal-Mart Stores, Inc. (2008b).
9. Wal-Mart Stores, Inc. (2008a).
10. Landrum (2008).
11. U.S. Census Bureau (2007).
12. Hillen (2007).
13. El Dorado Promise (2008).

Chapter 3

1. Retrieved January 30, 2009, from http://www.GreenJobInterview.com
2. Creamer Media (n.d.).
3. Creamer Media (n.d.).
4. Retrieved January 30, 2009, from https://www2.gotomeeting.com
5. Retrieved March 23, 2009, from http://www.gotowebinar.com
6. Svoboda and Whalen (2005).
7. LaMonica (2008); Murray (2008).
8. Jones (2008); O'Carroll (2008).
9. Bezdek (2009).
10. Retrieved January 28, 2009, from http://www.halogensoftware.com

11. Retrieved January 28, 2009, from http://www.empxtrack.com/performance -management-system

12. Retrieved March 25, 2009, from http://www.jeanpaulconsult.com/typical _topics.html#capacity

13. Retrieved January 28, 2009, from http://www.hr.com

14. Retrieved January 28, 2009, from http://salary.com

15. Retrieved January 28, 2009, from www.salarysource.com

16. Green Car Congress (2006).

17. American Express (2007).

18. Retrieved March 25, 2009, from http://www.chainleader.com/article/ CA6590430.html

Chapter 4

1. McKinsey & Company (2009).

2. McKinsey & Company (2009).

3. Frigo (2002).

4. Yachnin & Associates and Sustainable Investment Group Ltd. (2006).

5. Stagl (2007); International Finance Corporation CommDev (2009).

6. International Finance Corporation CommDev (2009).

7. Retrieved March 23, 2009, from http:///www.dsireusa.org

8. Retrieved March 23, 2009, from http://www.greenmoneyjournal.com

9. Retrieved March 23, 2009, from http://www.clear-profit.com

10. Social Investment Forum (2008).

11. Social Investment Forum (2007).

12. Retrieved March 23, 2009, from http://www.kld.com/indexes

13. Allianz Global Investors (2009).

14. Frigo (2002).

15. Frigo (2002).

16. Kaplan and Norton (1992).

17. Rigby and Bilodeau (2007).

18. Figge, Hahn, Schaltegger, and Wagner (2002); Moller and Schaltegger (2005); Radcliffe (1999).

19. Groupe Caisse d'Epargne (2008).

20. Strolling of the Heifers (2009).

21. Malhotra (2008).

22. Ward and Patterson (2003).

23. Ward and Patterson (2003).

24. Ernst & Young (2008).

25. Ernst & Young (2008).

26. Association of British Insurers (2005).

27. Mills (2007).

28. Tergesen (2008).

29. Bordoff (2008).

30. Ross, Mills, and Hecht (2007).

31. Makower (2005).

Chapter 5

1. McDonough and Braungart (2002).

2. McDonough Braungart Design Chemistry, LLC (2008).

3. Benyus (1997).

4. Benyus (1997).

5. Biomimicry Institute (2009).

6. Biomimicry Institute (2009).

7. WhalePower (n.d.).

8. Biomimicry Institute (2009).

9. Retrieved March 23, 2009, from http://www.asknature.org

10. Bhat (1996).

11. Gloria (2009).

12. Scientific Applications International Corporation (2006).

13. Scientific Applications International Corporation (2006).

14. Narayan and Patel (n.d.).

15. Vink (2007).

16. Athena Institute (2006).

17. Howe (2006).

18. Retrieved March 23, 2009, from http://www.yet2.com

19. Retrieved March 26, 2009, from http://www.crowdspring.com

20. Retrieved March 26, 2009, from https://www.mturk.com/mturk/welcome

Chapter 6

1. Manjumder and Groenevelt (2001).

2. Washington State University Extension Energy Program (n.d.).

3. Prahalad and Hart (2002).

4. Retrieved March 23, 2009, from http://archive.greenpeace.org/comms/97/summit/greenwash.html

5. Retrieved March 23, 2009, from http://www.terrachoice.com/Home/Six%20Sins%20of%20Greenwashing

6. Retrieved March 23, 2009, from http://www.corpwatch.org/article.php?list=type&type=102

7. Bruno (2002).

8. Retrieved March 23, 2009, from http://www.greenwashingindex.com

Chapter 7

1. McKinsey & Company (2008).
2. Global eSustainability Initiative (2008).
3. McKinsey & Company (2008).
4. Harrison (2008).
5. Condon (2009).
6. Naegel (2009).
7. Chua (n.d.).
8. Chua (n.d.).
9. Chua (n.d.).
10. Retrieved March 23, 2009, from http://www.epa.gov/epawaste/conserve/materials/ecycling/donate.htm

Chapter 8

1. Landrum, Daily, and Vjin (2009).
2. World Business Council for Sustainable Development and International Finance Corporation (2008).
3. World Resources Institute and World Business Council for Sustainable Development (2004, 2005).
4. World Business Council for Sustainable Development (2007).
5. Global Environmental Management Initiative (2002).
6. KPMG International (2008).
7. AccountAbility (2008).
8. International Federation of Accountants (2003).
9. AccountAbility (2005a, 2005b).
10. Kaplan and Cooper (1998).
11. Barringer (2003).
12. Kumaran, Ong, Tan, and Nee (2001).
13. Carter, Perruso, and Lee (2008).

Chapter 9

1. Friedman (1970).
2. Doering et al. (2002).
3. Cooperider (2008).
4. United Nations Global Compact (2008).
5. Endenburg (1998); Siong and Chen (2007); Buck and Villines (2007).
6. Landrum, Boje, and Gardner (2009); Rochlin and Googins (2005).
7. Landrum, Boje, et al. (2009).
8. Hamel and Prahalad (1990).

9. Hamel and Prahalad (1990).

10. Freeman (1984); Mitchell, Agle, and Wood (1997).

11. A. T. Kearney, Inc. (2009).

12. Deutsch (2005).

13. Landrum (2009).

14. Prahalad and Hart (2002).

15. Landrum (2007).

16. Simanis and Hart (2008).

17. Howe (2006).

18. Tapscott and Williams (2006).

Part II

1. Retrieved March 23, 2009, from http://www.alaffia.com; all Web sites in the following notes have been retrieved on March 23, 2009.

2. http://baabaazuzu.com

3. http://www.betterworldclub.com

4. http://www.betterworldtelecom.com

5. http://www.boulevardbread.com

6. http://www.boutiquemix.com

7. http://www.brilliantearth.com

8. http://www.burgerville.com

9. http://www.caracalla.com

10. http://www.cleanairlawncare.com

11. http://www.cleangreencollision.com

12. http://www.creativepaperwales.co.uk/index.asp

13. http://www.credomobile.com

14. http://www.earthclassmail.com

15. http://earthtones.com

16. http://www.ecocarwash.com

17. http://www.ecolibris.net

18. http://www.edunonline.com

19. http://www.edun-live.com

20. http://www.edunliveoncampus.com

21. http://www.fairtradesports.com

22. http://fio360.com

23. http://freerangestudios.com

24. http://frogsleap.com

25. http://www.gaianapavalleyhotel.com

26. http://www.galacticpizza.com

27. http://www.poopoopaper.com

28. http://www.greatlakesbrewing.com

29. http://www.thegreenmicrogym.com
30. http://www.greenforce.biz
31. http://www.greystonbakery.com
32. http://www.habanaoutpost.com
33. http://www.highergroundstrading.com
34. http://www.hopworksbeer.com
35. http://www.hotlipspizza.com
36. http://www.immaculatebaking.com
37. http://www.indigenousdesigns.com
38. http://www.icestone.biz
39. http://www.izzysicecream.com
40. http://www.keenfootwear.com
41. http://littlerockgreengarage.com
42. http://www.ljurban.com
43. http://www.pedaleadas.com
44. http://www.massanelliscleaners.com
45. http://www.naturalfusionhairstudio.com
46. http://www.peacecereal.com/index.html
47. http://www.pinehurstinn.com
48. http://www.pizzafusion.com
49. http://www.sweetriot.com
50. http://www.sunnightsolar.com
51. http://www.thanksgivingcoffee.com
52. http://tomsshoes.com
53. http://www.tropicalsalvage.com
54. http://www.verterra.com
55. http://www.wbfit.com
56. http://www.whitedog.com
57. http://www.zambezihoney.com

References

AccountAbility. (2005a). *Stakeholder engagement standard: Exposure draft.* Retrieved November 27, 2008, from http://www.accountability21.net/uploadedFiles/ publications/SES%20Exposure%20Draft%20-%20FullPDF.pdf

AccountAbility. (2005b). *From words to action: The stakeholder engagement manual, volume 2: The practitioner's handbook on stakeholder engagement.* Retrieved November 21, 2008, from AccountAbility, United Nations Environment Programme, and Stakeholder Research Associates Canada, Inc.: http://www .accountability21.net/uploadedFiles/publications/Stakeholder%20Engagement %20Handbook.pdf

AccountAbility. (2008). *AA1000 assurance standard 2008.* Retrieved May 23, 2009, from http://www.accountability21.net/uploadedFiles/publications/ AA1000AS%202008.pdf

Allianz Global Investors. (2009). *Press release: Nationwide survey finds: Americans see watershed era for environmental investing.* Retrieved February 14, 2009, from http://www.allianzinvestors.com/imageLibrary/promotions/EcoTrendsMedia/ index.html

American Express. (2007). *Careers: Diversity@work.* Retrieved February 25, 2009, from http://www10.americanexpress.com/sif/cda/page/0,1641,26482,00.asp

Association of British Insurers. (2005). *Financial risks of climate change: June 2005 summary report.* Retrieved February 2, 2009, from http://www.abi.org .uk/Display/File/Child/552/Financial_Risks_of_Climate_Change.pdf

Athena Institute. (2006). *Life cycle inventory of five products produced from polylactide (PLA) and petroleum-based resins.* Retrieved April 8, 2008, from http://www.athenasmi.ca/projects/docs/Plastic_Products_LCA_Summary _Rpt.pdf

Athena Sustainable Materials Institute. (2006). *Life cycle inventory of five products produced from polylactide (PLA) and petroleum-based resins: Technical report.* Retrieved April 8, 2008, from http://www.athenasmi.ca/projects/docs/Plastic _Products_LCA_Technical_Rpt.pdf

A. T. Kearney, Inc. (2009, February 9). *Press release: Companies with a commitment to sustainability tend to outperform their peers during the financial crisis.* Retrieved February 13, 2009, from http://www.atkearney.com/main .taf?p=1,5,1,223

Barakovic, A., Armato, B., Watson, C., Griffin, E., Tarter, W., & Ojeda, A. (2009). *UALR College of Business Paper Project*. Unpublished manuscript, University of Arkansas at Little Rock.

Barringer, H. P. (2003, May 20). *A life cycle cost summary*. Paper presented at the International Conference of Maintenance Societies (IOCMS), Perth, Australia. Retrieved February 12, 2009, from http://www.barringer1.com/pdf/LifeCycleCostSummary.pdf

Benyus, J. (1997). *Biomimicry: Innovation inspired by nature*. New York: HarperCollins.

Bezdek, R. (2009). *Green collar jobs in the U.S. and Colorado: Economic drivers for the 21st century*. Boulder, CO: American Solar Energy Society. Retrieved May 23, 2009, from http://www.greenforall.org/resources/ases-green-collar-jobs-report-forecasts-37-million-jobs-from-renewable-energy-and-energy-efficiency-in-u.s.-by-2030

Bhat, V. (1996). *The green corporation: The next competitive advantage*. Westport, CT: Quorum Books.

Biomimicry Institute. (2009). *Case studies*. Retrieved February 10, 2009, from http://www.biomimicryinstitute.org/case-studies/case-studies

Bordoff, J. (2008). Pay-as-you-drive car insurance. *Democracy Journal, 8*. Retrieved January 24, 2009, from http://www.brookings.edu/articles/2008/spring_car_insurance_bordoff.aspx

Brundtland, G. H. (Ed.). (1987). *Our common future: The World Commission on Environment and Development*. Oxford: Oxford University Press.

Bruno, K. (2002). *Greenwash + 10: The UN's Global Compact, corporate accountability and the Johannesburg Earth Summit*. Retrieved March 23, 2009, from CorpWatch: http://www.corpwatch.org/article.php?id=1348

Buck, J., & Villines, S. (2007). *We the people: Consenting to a deeper democracy*. Washington, DC: Sociocracy.info Press.

Carter, D., Perruso, L., & Lee, D. (2008). *Full cost accounting in environmental decision making* (University of Florida, IFAS Extension. Publication No. FE310). Retrieved February 12, 2009, from http://edis.ifas.ufl.edu/FE310

Chua, J. (n.d.). How to buy a green PC: An environmentally friendly computer will help preserve the environment—and save you money. *Computer Shopper*. Retrieved January 15, 2009, from http://computershopper.com/feature/how-to-buy-a-green-pc

Clean Air-Cool Planet. (2006). *A consumer's guide to retail carbon offset providers*. Retrieved December 13, 2008, from http://www.cleanair-coolplanet.org/ConsumersGuidetoCarbonOffsets.pdf

Condon, S. (2009, March 19). FTC questions cloud-computing security. *CNET News*. Retrieved March 24, 2009, from http://news.cnet.com/8301-13578_3-10198577-38.html

Cooperider, D. (2008, July/August). Sustainable innovation. *BizEd*. Retrieved December 12, 2008, from the Association for the Advancement of Collegiate Schools of Business: http://www.aacsb.edu/publications/Archives/JulAug08/32-39%20Sustainable%20Innovation.pdf

Creamer Media. (n.d.). *Video reduces Vodafone CO_2 Omissions [sic]*. Retrieved February 11, 2009, from http://llnw.creamermedia.co.za/articles/attachments/17588_vodafone.pdf

Deutsch, C. (2005, December 9). New surveys show that big business has a P.R. problem. *New York Times*, C 1. Retrieved February 13, 2009, from http://www.nytimes.com/2005/12/09/business/09backlash.html?_r=1&pagewanted=print

Doering, D., Cassara, A., Layke, C., Ranganathan, J., Revenga, C., Tunstall, D., et al. (2002). *Tomorrow's markets: Global trends and their implications for business*. Retrieved March 30, 2006, from the World Resources Institute, United Nations Environment Programme, and World Business Council for Sustainable Development: http://pdf.wri.org/tm_tomorrows_markets.pdf

El Dorado Promise. (2008, January 18). *El Dorado celebrates second anniversary of Promise scholarship program*. Retrieved March 3, 2008, from http://eldo.cjrwbeta.com/news/Story.aspx?storyID=4

Elkington, J. (1997). *Cannibals with forks: The triple bottom line of 21st century business*. Oxford: Capstone.

Endenburg, G. (1998). *Sociocracy: The organization of decision making*. Delft, Netherlands: Eburon Academic Publishers.

Ernst & Young. (2008). *Strategic business risk 2008: Insurance*. Retrieved February 14, 2009, from http://www.ey.com/Global/assets.nsf/International/Industry_Insurance_StrategicBusinessRisk_2008/$file/Industry_Insurance_StrategicBusinessRisk_2008.pdf

Figge, F., Hahn, T., Schaltegger, S., & Wagner, M. (2002). *The sustainability balanced scorecard—theory and application of a tool for value-based sustainability management*. Retrieved March 26, 2009, from http://www.cleanerproduction.com/SBS/SBC%20Theory%20and%20Appl%20-%20Figge.pdf

Freeman, R. E. (1984). *Strategic management: A stakeholder approach*. Boston: Pitman.

Friedman, M. (1970, September 13). The social responsibility of business is to increase its profits. *New York Times, SM17*. Retrieved February 14, 2009, from http://www.colorado.edu/studentgroups/libertarians/issues/friedman-soc-resp-business.html

Frigo, M. (2002). Nonfinancial performance measures and strategy execution. *Strategic Finance, 84*(2), 6–9.

Gardner, T. (2008). *First U.S. carbon auction brings states $39 mln*. Retrieved September 30, 2008, from Reuters: http://www.reuters.com/article/environmentNews/

idUSTRE48S48120080929?feedType=RSS&feedName=environmentNews
&pageNumber=1&virtualBrandChannel=0

Gerngross, T., & Slater, S. (2000). How green are green plastics? *Scientific American, 283*(2), 37–41. Retrieved April 8, 2008, from http://www.mindfully.org/Plastic/Biodegrade/Green-PlasticsAug00.htm

Global Environmental Management Initiative. (2002). *Connecting the drops toward creative water strategies: A water sustainability tool.* Washington, DC: Global Environmental Management Initiative. Retrieved October 20, 2008, from http://www.gemi.org/resources/ConnectingTheDrops.pdf

Global eSustainability Initiative. (2008). *SMART 2020: Enabling the low carbon economy in the information age.* Retrieved May 23, 2009, from http://www.gesi.org/files/smart2020report_lo_res.pdf

Gloria, T. (2009). *Life-cycle assessment.* Retrieved February 6, 2009, from http://www.life-cycle.org/LCA_soft.htm

Green Car Congress. (2006, December 11). Clif Bar launches cool commute program: Incentives for B100 and hybrids. *GreenCarCongress.com.* Retrieved May 23, 2009, from http://www.greencarcongress.com/2006/12/clif_bar_launch.html

Groupe Caisse d'Epargne. (2008, June). *Sustainable development labeling of banking products: Initial methodological approach, vol. 1.* Retrieved February 14, 2009, from http://www.utopies.com/docs/Methodo-general-juin2008light.pdf

Haag, T., Maloney, R., & Ward, J. (2006). *Paper or Styrofoam: A review of the environmental effects of disposable cups.* Retrieved February 16, 2009, from http://pspc.intoweb.co.za/UserFiles/pspc.intoweb.co.za//UCSD_Paper_or_Foam_report.pdf

Hamel, G., & Prahalad, C. K. (1990, May–June). The core competence of the corporation. *Harvard Business Review, 68*(3), 79–91.

Harrison, A. (2008). *Symantec energy efficient IT: Case studies.* Retrieved May 23, 2009, from http://www.symantec.com/content/en/us/enterprise/media/stn/pdfs/Articles/symantec_energy_efficient_data_center_case_studies.pdf

Hillen, M. (2007, May 27). 205 El Dorado seniors getting set to take on Promise's challenge. *Arkansas Democrat-Gazette.* Retrieved June 8, 2007, from LexisNexis.

Howe, J. (2006, June). The rise of crowdsourcing. *Wired.* Retrieved March 17, 2007, from http://www.wired.com/wired/archive/14.06/crowds.html

International Federation of Accountants. (2003). *ISAE 3000 (revised): Assurance engagements other than audits or reviews of historical financial information.* New York: International Auditing and Assurance Standards Board, International Federation of Accountants.

International Finance Corporation CommDev. (2009). *Sustainability investments in oil, gas & mining: Mitigating risk, delivering quality, increasing value.*

Retrieved March 23, 2009, from http://commdev.org/content/calendar/detail/2381

Jones, V. (2008). *The green collar economy: How one solution can fix our two biggest problems.* New York: HarperOne.

Kaplan, R., & Cooper, R. (1998). *Cost & effect.* Boston: Harvard Business School Press.

Kaplan, R., & Norton, D. (1992, January–February). The balanced scorecard: Measures that drive performance. *Harvard Business Review, 73*(7/8), 71–80.

Kollmuss, A., & Bowell, B. (2007). *Voluntary offsets for air-travel carbon emissions: Evaluations and recommendations of voluntary offset companies* (Rev. 1.3). Medford MA: Tufts Climate Initiative, Tufts University. Retrieved October 24, 2008, from http://www.tufts.edu/tie/carbonoffsets/TCI_Carbon_Offsets_Paper_April-2-07.pdf

KPMG International. (2008). *KPMG International survey of corporate responsibility reporting 2008.* Retrieved May 23, 2009, from http://us.kpmg.com/RutUS_prod/Documents/8/Corporate_Sustainability_Report_US_Final.pdf

Kumaran, S., Ong, S., Tan, R., & Nee, A. (2001). Environmental life cycle cost analysis of products. *Environmental Management and Health, 12,* 260–275. Retrieved February 12, 2009, from http://www.lcacenter.org/InLCA/pdf/4cKumaran.pdf

LaMonica, M. (2008, June 24). CleanLoop tackles clean-tech skills shortage. *CNET News.* Retrieved May 23, 2009, from http://news.cnet.com/8301-11128_3-9975946-54.html

Landrum, N. (2007). Advancing the "base of the pyramid" debate. *Strategic Management Review, 1*(1), 1–12.

Landrum, N. (2008). Murphy Oil and the El Dorado Promise: A case of strategic philanthropy. *Journal of Business Inquiry, 7*(1), 79–85.

Landrum, N. (2009). *Unintended consequences of business with 4 billion.* Manuscript submitted for publication (copy on file with author).

Landrum, N., Boje, D., & Gardner, C. (2009). *Applying an integral vision to strategic management: A model for integral strategy.* Manuscript submitted for publication (copy on file with author).

Landrum, N., Daily, C., & Vjin, S. (2009). *Corporate accountability: A path-goal perspective.* Manuscript submitted for publication (copy on file with author).

Lilienfeld, R. (2007). *Review of life cycle data relating to disposable, compostable, biodegradable, and reusable grocery bags.* Retrieved February 18, 2009, from http://www.deq.state.mi.us/documents/deq-ess-p2-recycling-PaperPlasticSummary_2.pdf

Makower, J. (2005, December 11). *Insurance and climate change: A matter of policy.* Retrieved February 2, 2009, from http://www.huffingtonpost.com/joel-makower/insurance-and-climate-cha_b_12083.html?view=print

Malhotra, H. (2008, August 4). *Fighting poverty one micro loan at a time. The Epoch Times.* Retrieved January 29, 2009, from http://www.theepochtimes.com/n2/business/fighting-poverty-one-micro-loan-at-a-time-2150.html.

Manjumder, P., & Groenevelt, H. (2001, Summer). Competition in remanufacturing. *Production and Operations Management.* Retrieved on March 26, 2009, from http://findarticles.com/p/articles/mi_qa3796/is_200107/ai_n8954853

McDonough Braungart Design Chemistry, LLC. (2008). *Cradle to cradle certification program,* version 2.1.1. Retrieved February 14, 2009, from http://www.mbdc.com/docs/Outline_CertificationV2_1_1.pdf

McDonough, W., & Braungart, M. (2002). *Cradle to cradle: Remaking the way we make things.* New York: North Point Press.

McKinsey & Company. (2008). *Revolutionizing data center efficiency.* Retrieved February 12, 2009, from http://www.mckinsey.com/clientservice/bto/pointofview/pdf/Revolutionizing_Data_Center_Efficiency.pdf

McKinsey & Company. (2009). *McKinsey global survey results: Valuing corporate social responsibility.* Retrieved March 23, 2009, from http://www.commdev.org/files/2393_file_McKQ_Valuing_Corporate_Social_Responsibility.pdf

Mills, E. (2007). *From risk to opportunity: 2007: Insurer responses to climate change.* Retrieved February 14, 2009, from http://www.climate-insurance.org/upload/pdf/Mills2007_Insurers_response_to_climate_change.pdf

Mitchell, R. K., Agle, B. R., & Wood, D. J. (1997). Toward a theory of stakeholder identification and salience: Defining the principle of who and what really counts. *Academy of Management Review, 22*(4), 853–886.

Moller, A., & Schaltegger, S. (2005). The sustainability balanced scorecard as a framework for eco-efficiency analysis. *Journal of Industrial Ecology, 9*(4), 73–83. Retrieved March 26, 2009, from http://www.wbcsd.org/DocRoot/DkiB0YxO9BdRq8NwMMBQ/JIE9-4_Schaltegger.pdf

Murray, J. (2008, June 10). Green execs to command ?80-k plus salaries. *BusinessGreen.com.* Retrieved May 23, 2009, from http://www.businessgreen.com/business-green/news/2218695/green-execs-command-80k-plus

Naegel, B. (2009). Energy efficiency: The new SLA. *GreenerComputing.com.* Retrieved January 15, 2009, from http://greenercomputing.com/feature/2009/01/13/energy-efficiency-the-new-sla

Narayan, R., & Patel, M. (n.d.). *Review and analysis of bio-based product LCA's.* Retrieved February 15, 2009, from http://www3.abe.iastate.edu/biobased/LCAreview.pdf

Obama for America. (2007). *Obama energy fact sheet.* Retrieved February 14, 2009, from http://obama.3cdn.net/4465b108758abf7a42_a3jmvyfa5.pdf

O'Carroll, E. (2008, July 29). Study: Green jobs could spark "explosive growth." *Christian Science Monitor.* Retrieved May 23, 2009, from http://features.csmonitor.com/environment/2008/07/29/study-green-jobs-could-spark-explosive-growth

Paster, P. (2006, September 11). Ask Pablo: The coffee mug debacle. *Triple Pundit*. Retrieved April 8, 2008, from http://www.triplepundit.com/pages/ask-pablo-the-c.php

Prahalad, C. K., & Hart, S. (2002). Fortune at the bottom of the pyramid. *strategy+business, 26*, 54–67.

Radcliffe, M. (1999). *Using the balanced scorecard to develop metrics for sustainable development.* Conference proceedings of Greening of Industry Network, Chapel Hill, NC.

Rigby, D., & Bilodeau, B. (2007). *Management tools and trends 2007.* Retrieved September 13, 2007, from http://www.bain.com/management_tools/Management _Tools_and_Trends_2007.pdf

Rochlin, S., & Googins, B. (2005). *The value proposition for corporate citizenship.* Boston: Center for Corporate Citizenship at Boston College.

Ross, C., Mills, E., & Hecht, S. (2007, Feb. 24). *Review of liability insurance considerations in the context of global climate change.* Retrieved May 22, 2009, from http://eetd.lbl.gov/emills/PRESENTATIONS/Insurance-Liability-Stanford.pdf

Scientific Applications International Corporation. (2006). *Life cycle assessment: Principles and practice.* Cincinnati, OH: National Risk Management Research Laboratory, Office of Research and Development, U.S. Environmental Protection Agency.

Simanis, E., & Hart, S. (2008). *The base of the pyramid protocol: Toward next generation BoP strategy* (2nd ed.). Ithaca, NY: Cornell University, Johnson School of Management, Center for Sustainable Global Enterprise. Retrieved February 13, 2009, from http://www.bop-protocol.org/docs/BoPProtocol2ndEdition2008.pdf

Siong, N., & Chen, G. (2007). *Dynamic governance: Embedding culture, capabilities and change in Singapore.* Singapore: World Scientific Publishing.

Social Investment Forum. (2007). *Performance and socially responsible management.* Retrieved January 25, 2009, from http://www.socialinvest.org/resources/performance.cfm

Social Investment Forum. (2008). *2007 report on socially responsible investing trends in the United States: Executive summary.* Retrieved May 23, 2009, from http://www.socialinvest.org/pdf/SRI_Trends_ExecSummary_2007.pdf

Stagl, S. (2007). *SDRN rapid research and evidence review on emerging methods for sustainability valuation and appraisal.* Retrieved March 23, 2009, from http://sdrnadmin.rechord.com/wp-content/uploads/sdrnemsvareviewfinal.pdf

Strolling of the Heifers. (2009). Retrieved February 14, 2009, from http://www.strollingoftheheifers.com/v2

Svoboda, S., & Whalen, J. (2005, October 19). *Using experiential simulation to teach sustainability.* Retrieved May 23, 2009, from Greenbiz.com: http://www.greenbiz.com/resources/resource/using-experiential-simulation-teach-sustainability

Tapscott, D., & Williams, A. (2006). *Wikinomics: How mass collaboration changes everything*. New York: Portfolio.

Tergesen, A. (2008, March 6). Insurance goes green. *Business Week*. Retrieved February 2, 2009, from http://www.businessweek.com/magazine/content/08_11/b4075072486226.htm?campaign_id=rss_daily.

United Nations Global Compact. (2008). *Overview of the UN Global Compact*. Retrieved January 21, 2009, http://www.unglobalcompact.org/aboutthegc/index.html

U.S. Census Bureau. (2007). *Annual estimates of the population for incorporated places in Arkansas*. Retrieved April 2, 2008, from http://www.census.gov/popest/cities/tables/SUB-EST2006-04-05.xls

Vink, E. (2007). *Reducing the environmental footprint of NatureWorks® polymer*. Retrieved February 18, 2009, from http://www.lcm2007.org/presentation/Mo_2.04-Vink.pdf

Wal-Mart Stores, Inc. (2008a). *Sustainability fact sheet*. Retrieved December 13, 2008, from http://walmartstores.com/ViewResource.aspx?id=2392

Wal-Mart Stores, Inc. (2008b). *Wal-Mart launches green jobs council*. Retrieved December 13, 2008, from http://walmartstores.com/FactsNews/NewsRoom/8835.aspx

Ward, D., & Patterson, J. (2003, November 10). Community development venture capital. *WTN News*. Retrieved January 24, 2009, from http://wistechnology.com/articles/339

Washington State University Extension Energy Program. (n.d.). *Idling restrictions*. Retrieved February 15, 2009, from http://www.energy.wsu.edu/documents/renewables/IdlingRestrictions.pdf

WhalePower. (n.d.). Retrieved January 30, 2009, from http://www.whalepower.com/drupal

World Business Council for Sustainable Development. (2007). *The global water tool*. Geneva, Switzerland: Author. Retrieved October 20, 2008, from http://www.wbcsd.org/templates/TemplateWBCSD5/layout.asp?type=p&MenuId=MTUxNQ&doOpen=1&ClickMenu=LeftMenu=LeftMenu

World Business Council for Sustainable Development and International Finance Corporation. (2008). *Measuring impact*. Retrieved October 20, 2008, from http://www.wbcsd.org/templates/TemplateWBCSD5/layout.asp?type=p&MenuId=MTU3Mw

World Resources Institute and World Business Council for Sustainable Development. (2004). *The Greenhouse Gas Protocol: A corporate accounting and reporting standard* (Rev. ed.). Washington, DC: Author. Retrieved May 23, 2009, from http://www.ghgprotocol.org/files/ghg-protocol-revised.pdf

World Resources Institute and World Business Council for Sustainable Development. (2005). *The Greenhouse Gas Protocol: The GHG Protocol for project accounting.* Washington, DC: Author. Retrieved May 23, 2009, from http://www.ghgprotocol.org/files/ghg project_protocol.pdf

Yachnin & Associates and Sustainable Investment Group Ltd. (2006). *The sdEffect: Translating sustainable development into financial valuation measures: A pilot analytical framework.* Retrieved March 23, 2009, from http://www.sdeffect.com/sdEffectFeb2006.pdf;

Index

Note: The italicized *f* and *t* following page numbers refer to figures and tables, respectively.